CULTURE BASED PERFORMANCE

How CEOs and Leaders can Co-create High Performing Teams and Sustainable Growth

To Nic
So excited to see how the future unfolds. Hope you enjoy the book

DR. CARI LEYSHON &

DR. JACQUELINE HIDDLESTONE-MUMFORD

TESTIMONIALS

This book offers valuable insights on a range of perspectives around both individual and organisational culture. For what seems a small shift in thinking at times can make a large impact on both our day-to-day lives and an organisation's continued viability. Work your way through the chapters and exercises, reflect on the thinking scenarios and discover how the combination is a key to your success.

Juanita Illingworth
Snr Professor, France

Dr. Cari and Dr. Jacqui have created a roadmap for embedding Agility Ability into your organisational culture to make Cultural inQuiry part of your business DNA. Read with an open mind and you will see how the sustainable culture reset strategy will benefit you.

Janine LeaBarrett
Founder and Director, Advisory Board NED, Australia

Working with Dr. Cari and Dr. Jacqui made our team more aware of small individual and cultural differences. Clear communication on expectations and explanation of the meaning of words and terms made a huge difference to our day-to-day life at the office. The perfect proof that small changes can make a big difference.

Karolien Dockers
CEO, Belgium

I had the chance to work with Dr. Cari and Dr. Jacqui on a project concerning the 'Connexx European Enforcement Network'. It was a real pleasure to work with them. Especially their ideas and the dedication they put into this project was extraordinary. The result being that Connexx now has a member service charter. Dr. Cari was able to guide us towards this result without imposing but by making suggestions in order to reach our end.

Geoffrey Galle
Enforcement Officer, Chairman Connexx Enforcement Network

CULTURE BASED PERFORMANCE

How CEOs and Leaders can Co-create High Performing Teams and Sustainable Growth

DR. CARI LEYSHON &
DR. JACQUELINE HIDDLESTONE-MUMFORD

COPYRIGHT

Paperback ISBN: 978-3-9525916-1-1
Hardcover ISBN: 978-3-9525916-0-4

Authors: Dr. Cari Leyshon and Dr. Jacqueline Hiddlestone-Mumford.

Publisher: CQify Publishing
Publication date: 2023

Email: info@cqify.com

Address: CQify GmbH, Krummenrainweg 69, CH-4153, Reinach, Switzerland

Website: www.cqify.com

Please direct all enquiries to the authors.

DEDICATED TO

our family, friends, colleagues, the CQify team, our relentless community of supporters, and everyone who strives to be the best version of themselves

CONTENTS

FOREWORD

This book offers CEOs and leaders valuable insights to inspire a fresh perspective about the value of being a co-creator and how this role influences organisational performance. The key insight this book offers, from my view, is how the learning journey unfolds from an individual perspective into co-creating a high performing team. A particular highlight is the approach used to help people understand their own cultural conditioning and influences. The outcomes show how a small shift can make a significant impact both on our day-to-day lives and within our organisation.

I was drawn to how our personal awareness of our individual or 'balloon head' barriers are preventing many of us from being effective in our roles. This book is a significant step forward towards a greater understanding of ourselves and others. Developing the agility of becoming a 'co-creator' of our personal and professional contribution will enhance any organisation's sustainable future, large or small. Embedding the learning through self-reflection aims to maintain and improve that agility.

As a fellow scholar-practitioner with Dr. Cari and Dr. Jacqui, I have found that the combination of their depth of experience and research provides a unique perspective. This book is designed for those 'edge walker' CEOs and leaders who are ready for the next level of personal and organisational development.

I find many links between this book and my research focused on glocalisation[1] within a multinational company. My investigation of conflicting perspectives around culture, linguistic and governance issues highlighted the importance of glocal dynamics, an aspect that resonates with the central insights in this book.

Glocalisation is a new reality every business leader needs to be considering. This book provides an essential roadmap showing how to embed Cultural inQuiry for organisational *Agility Ability*. I believe that CEOs and leaders would benefit greatly from the 'critical friend' concept. This is an independent conversation to challenge thinking, offering a sounding board that is both based on experience and relevant research, and definitely worthy of further exploration.

I invite you to join this journey to become a co-creator for yourself, your team, and your organisation. I am sure you will find this book as action provoking as I have.

Dr. Dermot Kennedy[1]

Senior Director, Global Web Production, Adobe

---

[1] *Footnote:* Dr. Kennedy focused on glocalisation in his doctoral thesis....and is in the process of developing a number of papers from his scholar-practitioner research.

His thesis is titled: Kennedy, D. (2021) 'Investigating conflicting perspectives at a software multinational concerning its efforts to produce culturally and linguistically appropriate web content for its customers around the globe', *UK: The University of Liverpool.*

INTRODUCTION

Are you that curious leader who is an early adopter, looking for a new innovative way to overcome the barriers preventing you from implementing your organisational plans?

Do you know what it takes to co-create a culture for high performing teams that can thrive on changes that arise due to a complex environment?

Are you wondering how to inspire more creativity and connection within your team?

If you have answered yes to any or all of these questions, you are in the right place.

This book aims to redefine how to embed an inclusive and agile organisational culture that embraces glocal[1] (those globally local) citizens. We aim to **advance** the concept of leadership, communication, emotional and cultural intelligence. If you haven't heard about cultural intelligence yet don't worry, we will share more about how it originated and where it is heading.

We will offer new evidence-based insights aimed at opening up or widening your current perspective about why co-creating your organisational culture is a sustainable ethos.

We are sharing a new perspective that deconstructs current views about leadership development, decision making, sustainable strategy implementation; and diversity, equity, inclusion and belonging (DEIB) thinking.

These concepts, views and perspectives have been developed based on our practical experience combined with foundational research conducted by Dr. Cari. To this foundation, Dr. Jacqui contributed further research and practical experiences to enhance the development of our CQify project. The CQify core team will continue to co-create ongoing development. The true source of creativity is always a collective effort where multiple perspectives drive value creation. This is our aim for you as the reader.

We invite you to join us on the discovery journey that will share how our individual cultural conditioning is impacting human-to-human connection. The role of our individual cultural identities is often overlooked in common business practice. We will share why cultural identities is an important aspect of people management. Plus, how this contributes to potential psychological barriers such as our social masks, fear, and ego. This new way of thinking and associated perspectives can potentially reduce barriers in all aspects of the organisation where there is human-to-human interaction.

Responsive human-to-human interaction is the sweet spot of reaching your full potential as a person, as a team, and as an organisation.

A key concept that we discuss is about upskilling conventional leadership to evolve the sole leader practices at the top to become co-creators - shifting from '**ME**' to '**WE**'.

Organisations need to be innovative but are currently struggling to achieve these objectives due to relentless day-to-day distractions.

What we know for sure is that:

- Creativity is a key to Innovation.
- Innovation is a key to Agility.
- Agility is a key to Next Level Performance....

So, the time is now to **Co-create** your **Organisational Agility Ability**™.

In the last section we share an evidence-based roadmap so you can start implementing a sustainable culture reset strategy that can flow with any form of ongoing complexity, including the ongoing development of technology.

This book introduces the competitive advantage of achieving agility ability™ for the whole organisation. This is the co-creator paradigm for organisational success.

We have developed the pioneering insight-led **Cultural inQuiry Cycles**© to create the optimal:

CULTURE-BASED PERFORMANCE™ for any type of organisation and all leaders.

This is where real sustainable change happens.

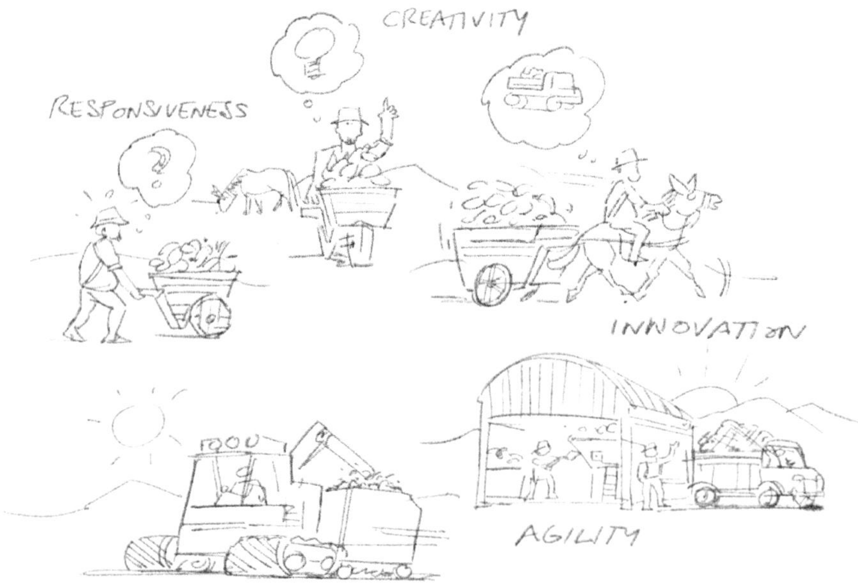

Interested to learn more?

This book takes a different approach in helping understand what is affecting businesses today by integrating multiple perspectives. As you already know, countries and continents have transitioned into a global village. Our journey illuminates the insanity of the quest and ongoing search for a solution to business problems that is still rooted in conventional thinking. These types of solutions were very helpful in the past, but we have new challenges and issues that require a fresh way of thinking.

What this means is we need to reconsider how organisations are interpreting the learning gained from their experience. Even more important is to understand where they are getting or sourcing their knowledge from.

Leaders are continuing to invest significant funds and spend valuable time doing what they have done historically to try to solve both current and new problems. This approach can be potentially self-defeating.

Today's reality requires new insights and a fresh way of looking at problems.

This book reviews the value of creating and sharing knowledge by embedding a learning culture within the team. Leaders are realising that learning or training sessions are no longer something that should only happen a few times per year. They are realising learning is essential for an organisation to inspire ongoing creativity. We are sure these are words or phrases you are used to hearing or have even said, 'sorry our training budget will not allow this' OR 'we only allocate training for our sales department (or whatever department)', not for the whole organisation. Even when education is offered to everyone, it is something that is attended versus an integrated part of their day-to-day activities. A learning culture is a customer centric earning culture.

In the world today, given the current problems developing in a dynamic environment, the complexities of work have grown significantly. This is the consensus. It is virtually impossible to plan and apply a detailed solution to any type of problem faced today, given the minute-by-minute change in the prevailing circumstances that makes long held assumptions potentially flawed. A level of agility is required to navigate the continual changing environment.

A vital issue is that by the time you or your research and development (R&D) department research the problem and then agree on the way forward, time goes on and the problem grows into something different. For example, you think you have a problem within your sales department, so you start implementing a training program to help improve the team's skills. Then later you discover that the sales manager is too direct and offending some of the team members. In general, the whole team is just not getting along. Then the issue has evolved to a team building, communication, or a leadership issue. Identifying the true source of a problem can be a big challenge for leaders. It can almost be like trying to staple jelly to a wall.

The good news is that our established ***LENS Framework***™ (**L**everaging culture to, **E**ngage, **N**on-judgmental insights, for **S**trategy implementation) helps modern day businesses propel problem solving above the conventional way of thinking. In other words, we need to take a different route to solve the challenges that organisations are facing. We aim to offer a series of robust insights for leaders to realise the importance and value in actively seeking ways to overcome challenges by finding the relevant answers to vital questions.

This overall process we outline throughout the book will stimulate an environment where employees experience psychological safety. That means they will feel confident and comfortable enough to contribute their ideas and insights. This could create opportunities to discover additional avenues for growth and development. Further results that can be possible is an increase in creativity, conscious engagement, collective decision making, agility, wellbeing, connection, improved retention rates, and overall collaborative productivity.

This book also emphasises the important role of a new leadership and management paradigm to ensure the implementation of the proposed plans. We share how to co-create high performing teams that will support those plans with the necessary resources.

Organisations are struggling to implement their plans, which is having a negative impact by limiting their growth and innovation. We cannot emphasise enough just how urgent this is to fix. Plans are only impactful once they are implemented, or it can restrict performance capabilities. We aim to provide an opportunity to reimagine how people can connect, teams can collaborate, and organisations can thrive.

Before we continue, it is important to keep an eye out for this symbol throughout the book CQ®. It highlights key insights, research, definitions, and other items we think will be helpful to point out.

We further added several CQ Thinking Scenarios, designed as thinking or insight / inQuiry tools to add clarity to the discussion being covered. We encourage you to jot down key points and any insights you may have as a result. This is where the use of a reflection journal is valuable as part of your personal development. Of course, this is all completely optional and for you to decide what is best for you.

This book has been laid out in parts that all work together to guide your reading and learning. To reset your organisation's culture, we will be focusing on the three agilities – inner, team, and organisational agility.

In Part One, we begin with the **CQ Inner Agility.** This is the *discovery* phase that offers the foundation to uncover the hidden potential inside yourself. This discovery process helps you to better understand yourself, your team, and your organisation, and how they fit together. It offers insights on how we think as individuals, our cultural influences, and the impact of our different perspectives on our lives and on others.

In Part Two, we move onto the **CQ Team Agility**. This is the *deep dive* phase that builds on the foundations of Part One to take the hidden potential inside us to the next level and apply that across our team. Deep dive also helps to understand how the differing perspectives and cultural influences of each team member needs to create high functioning teams in attaining Team Agility.

Part Three develops this further to **CQ Organisational Agility.** This is the *delivery* phase, the roadmap to move from inner agility, towards team agility, and onto organisational agility. We will take you on a series of phases that create greater insights about how to reset your organisational culture to deliver greater engagement, learning and overall co-created productive results.

The three parts culminate into organisational ***agility ability***™, to provide the capability of dealing with the complexities of the world today and tomorrow. Around these parts in the book, we add this introduction, and an additional section on case studies to support the progress through the parts.

We draw your attention to Part Three, where we offer a roadmap and information on how to directly apply **Cultural inQuiry**™ using our **LENS Framework**™ and **Cultural inQuiry Cycles**© to develop co-creating high performing teams. These insights will provide a guide that identifies how to connect the unique cultural dimensions of employees within an organisation to enable effective communication and collaboration. This co-created culture is the essence of your organisation's future. It is written with the aid of extensive research that aims to bridge the gaps between the current theory and advancing practice of leading and managing people in all types of organisations.

Within this book, we, Dr. Cari Leyshon (Dr. Cari) and Dr. Jacqueline Hiddlestone-Mumford (Dr. Jacqui), will take you on a journey of transitioning from ***me*** to ***we*** in enhancing your ***agility ability***™ - as we take a leap from individualism to co-creation within organisations. We help you focus on co-creating a culture-based performing team.

Let's get started!

PART ONE

INNER AGILITY

CHAPTER ONE
REPLACING JUDGEMENT WITH CURIOSITY AND HUMILITY

What would happen in your work environment if we all replaced judgement with curiosity and humility? Or, if we swapped being critical of ourselves and others for more compassion? How would this affect your relationships, both at work and in your personal life?

Now more than ever before, organisations need to be on the edge of driving innovation to embrace ongoing change by co-creating high performance teams within an agile working ecosystem. An ecosystem refers to external partners that assist each other with creating value and efficiency. These 'partnerships' nurture or influence the organisational offerings as a whole to help scale and implement value creation for everyone involved.

What this essentially means is that it is difficult for leaders to keep up with new technologies, and with all the advancement, operational hurdles are getting higher. For us, the evidence is clear, we are entering a new era where the focus must be on the quality of human-to-human communication and connection.

We all know that agility is essential for high performing teams, but what is really preventing your agility ability?

Thinking about your work environment for a moment, do you think that the plans made by yourself, or the leadership team ever get fully implemented? In most cases the answer is no, based on our research findings[5,6,7,8,46,56]. There is consistent research findings about plans, often referred to as strategies, that are developed with all the excitement of a new direction, new potential. Only that once they are completed, they are then placed on the shelf or in a drawer and not taken to the next level of implementation. Some are revisited and revived, others replaced with higher priorities as business-as-usual takes over or new challenges are faced.

To explore this on a deeper level we will explain the common barriers that prevent most businesses from implementing their plans or implementing them fully.

We will evolve this into a discussion on how to shift from being reactive to responsive when it comes to leadership, communication, decision making and facing business challenges.

Then we will show you how Cultural inQuiry™ **can** take your business to the **next level**.

This book is written in a way that is similar to peeling back the layers of an onion to get to the core of what is preventing leaders from implementing their plans.

The core of what is preventing full plan implementation is what we refer to as a lack of AGILITY ABILITY™. We want to work with you to attain your Agility Ability™ to achieve plan implementation and co-creating the organisational direction.

Let's deep dive into THE REAL PROBLEM

The recurring problem identified by our research is that many companies are struggling to put their plans into action[7,8,46,56].

These plans can also be called strategies. We prefer to say plans to keep it simple because there are all kinds of different meanings for strategies.

There can be all sorts of plans, for example: to improve technology, attract new customers, retain and attract key team members, improve the supply chain, or any other aspect for the business.

Failure to implement plans cause missed opportunities for overall performance, innovation, creativity, and agility.

Conversations that we have had with a variety of C-suite executives, such as CEOs, CFOs, and COOs, all repeat and share the same or similar concerns.

> While we focus only on the business-as-usual to the detriment of long-term deliverables, we miss the opportunities to break new ground and anchor our organisational future. Too many organisations go out of business this way.
>
> *Dr. Jacqui*

Every day, new issues and priorities arise that take a leader's focus away from necessary tasks related to implementing plans. This could be something crucial to the organisation like a key member of staff leaving the organisation, problems within the supply chain; or an ongoing, even one-off issue such as conflict between any groups of stakeholders, or any other form of 'emergency' or 'urgency'. When such urgent issues arise, it is easy to be caught up in solving the issue at hand, and everything else becomes secondary. These types of issues need to be addressed with some urgency since it is these distractions that are ongoing and perpetuating concerns.

From a neuroscience perspective, when unexpected events happen to us that can cause us stress or anxiety, our brain automatically goes into fight or flight mode. This is very helpful when you are being chased by a bear or a lion, but when it is happening to us daily our minds cannot cope with this level of fear, uncertainty and not knowing. This natural neurological process is instantly causing us to be reactive to the situations we are facing. This is when the part of the brain called the amygdala is triggered by any perceived threats we can assess, creating a fight or flight reaction.

The real issue is that we are all distracted and preoccupied with our heads full of busy thoughts about our 'to do' lists, fears around our jobs, relationships, boss's expectations, children, finances, future, past, health concerns, and so on.

Every day we are bombarded with potential solutions to our problems and overwhelmed with potential transformational solutions that never really work or that we can even make the necessary time for. We may pause and discover, or not even realise, that we are on the treadmill of life that goes nowhere fast. This ongoing cycle only perpetuates our problems and increases our stress levels. When we are feeling overwhelmed, stressed, time pressured or tired, we tend to stay stuck in a reactive mode.

Dr. Cari's research[5] identified several common barriers such as fear, our social masks, and our egos that keep us in a reactive mode:

1. Fear and fear-based thinking

The invisible individual psychological barrier such as ***fear*** of:

- Not being good enough,
- People not liking me,
- Asking questions,
- Losing a job,
- Not knowing the answers in meetings,
- Not smart enough,
- Saying or doing the wrong thing,
- Unsure of how to best answer a question in an interview,
- ....and the list goes on.

Fear can be seen by others as lack of confidence by the actions taken, comments made and general demeanour. To us, fear can be perceived as paralysing and prevents us from moving out of our comfort zone of what we know and are familiar with. It is mainly triggered by uncertainty or when something or someone is different from what we do or who we are. Our minds are constantly calculating situations and people around us to assess the perceived threat levels to our wellbeing.

The difficult part of how we view fear is that it comes from our social and cultural conditioning. Often it is easy to overlook how our cultural conditioning can contribute to these psychological barriers we are experiencing. Many people have never considered how our culture identity is directly linked to forming and influencing our perceptions about how we see the world. Even more interesting is that most people are not even consciously aware of how fear is limiting their worldview or experience of the world.

Now keeping in mind that some fears are actually very useful for our safety. For example, some fears prevent us from doing destructive or dangerous things. In this sense these would be considered helpful fears to have. The ones we are referring to are more about the limiting beliefs.

This and the ad hoc exercises, as with the Thinking Scenarios, throughout the book are optional. They aim to offer an opportunity to pause and reflect on the topic of discussion. Some readers take this approach, others return later to do them, and others read and move on. Feel free to take the approach that suits you.

CQ Exercise:

Take a moment to ask yourself the question:

Is fear limiting my life experience and if so, how?

At this point, for those wishing to proactively engage with the exercise, we recommend taking a journal or notebook and pen/s; even electronically works. Although we do find the tactility of a notebook used as a journal works best as you can refer back to it, add, doodle, and reflect on your decisions, thinking and learning. We both find that it is during these quiet moments that clarity emerges and new insights become clear.

CQ Exercise:

Take a moment and reflect on your answers.

Write them down.

Are they creating a social mask that you present to the world?

This is a great time to start thinking about your answers and how your fears can cause you to create a social mask that you then present to the world. It is only when you can acknowledge your fears that you can consider approaches to address them.

2. Our social mask

Our ***social mask*** is also created by our cultural and social conditioning. This is where we only feel that it is safe to bring certain aspects of ourselves to work but keep other parts hidden that we perceive will not be accepted by others. This can be the beginning of many misunderstandings, bad thoughts, and feelings of exclusion.

In today's world, social masks are going to the next level as we can replace ourselves as avatars in video communications and social media. We attended a meeting to present some ideas and everyone on the meeting was using an animal avatar. To be fair we found the situation amusing on the one hand, but then on the other it was really challenging not seeing the expressions on the participants faces. In our experience this really adds to the barriers of our ability to deeply connect and communicate, which we discuss this further in the book.

Our intention to try to cover parts of our identity, which can also be reinforced by our colleagues and leaders who say *'bring your whole self to work'* but then their non-verbal behaviour says *'except that part'* after seeing something they are judgemental of or don't personally accept. This is when our own unconscious perceptions, judgements and stereotypes can come into play automatically without our awareness.

When we hide behind our social ***masks*** and try to provide the impression that we think others prefer to hear or see, we become vulnerable to their acceptance. When we are trying to impress others or be accepted, we will pretend to like or be whatever is required to achieve these subjective needs. It is important to share that when we are seeking acceptance, we will be ready to constantly adapt ourselves to others' expectations.

When we can become aware of these illusions and stay true to our authentic selves, we can experience a deep sense of peace by being ourselves and not out of alignment just to please others. This is where we can begin to let go of attachments of things or behaviours that are no longer serving us.

This acknowledgement provides a shift towards feeling a sense of belonging that comes from the inner confidence that our differences are the treasures that make each of us shine. This is when we can become courageously curious to learn more about ourselves and others.

3. Our ego

First, we want to share, our ***ego*** is not the enemy. We need our ego to protect us and survive in the world.

Based on resilience psychology, our ego is considered unpredictable and needs to be checked on regularly to see if we are really aware of our true intentions and truth versus telling ourselves something believable to make us right. Our ego can sometimes trick us into thinking our way is the only way, believing it is protecting us from pain, harm, or conflict. When we automatically believe our ego, we are potentially closing ourselves off to new information or perspectives. In general, we are all vulnerable to our 'ego flare ups'. The difference is knowing how to recognise this state of mind and how to navigate it, which will be discovered as you continue reading.

To calm our ego, we need to guide it as opposed to being blindly led by it. This is a skill that requires ongoing awareness and rarely gets mastered.

The ego-led leader will:

- Avoid listening to others,

- Try to micro-manage or control,
- Use fear to intimidate,
- Have a general belief that their way is the best and only way,
- Stubbornly refuse to acknowledge different views.

The ego-led or ego-dominated leader was, at one time, considered the ultimate definition of being a successful leader. This was when life was more predictable, change could be 'planned' for, where creativity took a back seat to the main goal of being productive and squeezing every ounce of performance out of every team member with no consideration for their mental health or wellbeing. It was all about show up, do what you're told, keep your numbers up or you will be fired. The boss had the answers, had all the information, and made the important decisions. The world has changed, and leadership needs to, and has in some aspects, changed with it.

Have you ever experienced being managed by an ego-led leader, or our version of a CEO with a dominant ego, what we call a **C-EgO™**? Or do you think it is possible at times that you may even be one yourself?

Thinking Scenario
Alex

Alex didn't really want to go on the CQify training. He thought that he didn't need it. However, Alex was very moved by the description of the CEgO. He saw himself in the CEgO cartoon and felt pretty uncomfortable about it. He realised that he lost his temper far too easily at home as well as at work. He thought everyone was just disrespecting him – it didn't occur to Alex that his colleagues and family just had different thoughts about life to him.

Alex was really shocked to discover that his angry thinking had been firing up his amygdala for years and that explained why he would suddenly lose his temper for what seemed like very little reason. It made sense. He saw that he could give himself and everyone else a break if he remembered that no one else can think exactly like him – that's not possible. Alex had the insight that we are each living in our own separate thought created reality. He saw that he didn't have to force everyone to always agree with him. Indeed, even if others agreed, they may be masking their true thoughts just to keep the peace!

Alex decided to enjoy making his life easier by not fighting little things. He could see that others innocently just do what they think is right and that he did not always have to label their behaviours as wrong. It certainly helped his stress levels to be a bit more open minded...

Shifting from an ego-led leader (or C-EgO™) to a Co-creator

The next phase is to overcome these psychological barriers of fear, social mask, and ego. First, we need to acknowledge them by being aware that they even exist in the first place. If we don't understand what they are then it is impossible to recognise them within us. If they are left to run wild within us, we will remain stuck in a mode of reaction, just like being in a hamster wheel.

Once we can reflect and recognise these barriers, we will be able to shift from being reactive to situations to responsive. But what is the difference?

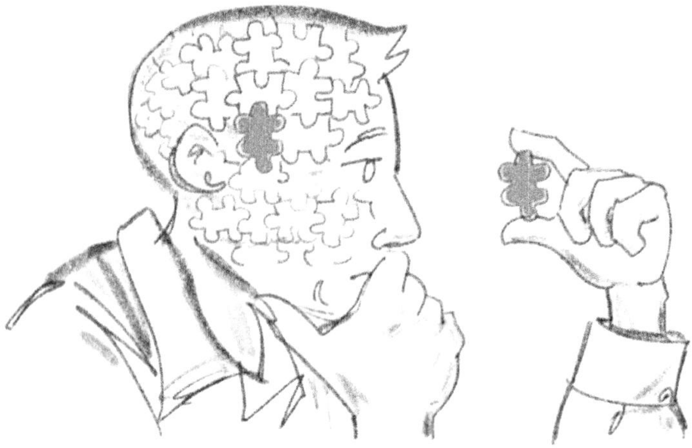

Here it is worth noting and reinforcing what our **'schema'** is. Our schema is our stereotypical thoughts. We need to acknowledge we have individual beliefs, judgements, stereotypes, and biases that make up our schema. We will use the word schema throughout the book. It is recommended that you take note of this definition to avoid confusion later about what it means.

What does it mean to be responsive instead of reactive?

We invite you to click on the QR code to the right to view a short video of what it means to be reactive versus responsive.

As you can see from the video, we are all balloon heads, preoccupied with our own problems, worries and troubles. No wonder we have conflicts and misunderstandings between our colleagues, bosses, and any other human in our lives. We are all experiencing floods of distractions that are fuelling our emotional reactions. When we are reactive, our emotions are steaming ahead in nano seconds before we even realise what is happening. Most of the time we are triggered emotionally before we know why.

Almost every single thought we are thinking can contribute to just making our *balloon head* larger and larger until we can no longer see our faces or anyone else's. We become absorbed with our own internal thoughts. Our minds become very busy, and we are unable to be truly aware of the responses and needs of ourselves and others. It's as if we get lost in the excessive thinking of our overactive minds. Then immediately we begin to FEEL our own THINKING. This is why in our video the bodies became the same colour as the balloon head.

Once we are feeling our thinking, this also triggers our actions or behaviours. Again, this happens instantaneously. We are actually stuck living in the toxicity of worry, stress, and fear, which shows up in our body and continues in this feedback loop on repeat. This is where we can dip into long-term depression, or even addiction. We are all normally acting out of our feelings, like 'I was thinking angry thoughts, so I shouted and then kicked the door' or 'When the boss said that last criticising remark, I just broke into uncontrollable tears'.

For example, you can walk into work late and your boss gives you 'that look', your balloon head fills up with a million thoughts, you automatically think the worst, become angry that they never even gave you a chance to explain, so you turn around to leave and slam the door. Meanwhile, moments before, your boss just had a call from the owner saying production is down and she needs to sort out her team or she will be fired. This instantly blew up her balloon head making it impossible to see that you were even upset. The cycle continues like a domino effect from person to person throughout the organisation.

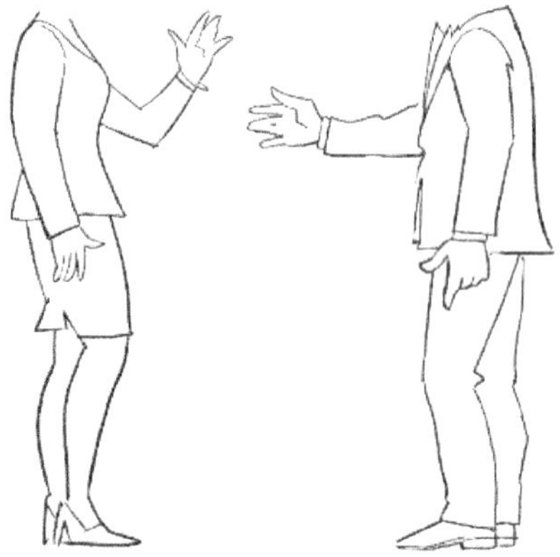

When everyone has a full balloon head, it is impossible to experience compassion or empathy for others as we can't see past our own balloon.

When we are in this state of mind, it is impossible for us to access our creativity. If we cannot be creative, there is no innovation, which is the main barrier to agility.

Thinking Scenario
Amir

Amir had found it difficult to begin a new project because he had been given a client that was known to have been demanding and short tempered. Amir spent so much time thinking about how the client might or might not react to his ideas. He was overthinking things and therefore had no mental space for new creative ideas of his own. His "balloon head" was full of stories he had heard about the client's previous demanding behaviour.

Amir found it helpful to recognise that he was mentally playing through scenarios of things that the client might say or do in the future. He saw he was living in the feeling of his thoughts about the client's potential disapproval. Clearly, it wasn't the client that was making him anxious, it was his thinking about the client in each moment!

Amir found it helpful to see that when we spend all our time trying to understand someone else's perspective we start to lose our capacity for our own fresh thinking.

He had some more insights, such as:

- What if I just let go of getting it perfectly right and just try a few ideas out?
- I can ask the team to give me some initial thoughts before proceeding further.
- We can try to co-create rather than me just working on my own with this...

- If I produce something they don't like that is because they have a separate reality to me ... it doesn't mean that I can't learn from their feedback and adapt accordingly.

Following those insights, Amir realised that by labelling the client "difficult" before meeting them he had created some blocks towards the client before they had even had a chance to work together. He said to himself, "I have created a fictional client in my head and I'm believing my thoughts about them... no wonder I am having a problem with creating some ideas for their campaign". Letting go of this thinking allowed Amir to focus on creating ideas for their campaign.

Needless to say, by having some insights like these Amir was able to respond better to the client brief. He could actually enjoy the creative process, regardless of how the client may react.

Similarly, when we don't fire the amygdala up by believing our catastrophising thinking, we can have some more helpful thinking. This in turn means we can rely on our common sense in the moment.

Thinking Scenario
Joanna

Joanna had spent ages creating a PowerPoint for a big presentation to her team. She had practiced it several times with her co-presenter. However, the night before the presentation she started to worry about what might happen in the presentation.

The image of the CQify "balloon head people" came into her mind. So, she decided to write down some of the thoughts that were filling her mind - here are just a few of them:

- What if I make a mistake or forget something?
- They are going to think am stupid.
- If I get this wrong, I won't get a promotion.
- The PowerPoint might freeze or the technology might not work.
- I'm not good enough for this and I'm gonna make a fool of myself.
- My boss has put her trust in me and I'm gonna let her and the team down.

She saw how each of these thoughts was a stressful one and would likely be firing up her amygdala in each moment as she was thinking them.

Then Joanna had a big insight - she really understood that it wasn't the presentation that was scaring her. It was the thoughts about the presentation that she was innocently thinking and believing which were making her feel anxious. Here, she was feeling sick and palms sweating, but she wasn't at the presentation – she was actually on her sofa at home.

Joanna realised that she really didn't have to believe all her old culturally conditioned thoughts about possible failure, and she found herself laughing out loud. She was a bit nervous the next day, but her insights were enough for her to calm down considerably. Of course, as her thoughts slowed down her feelings of panic weren't so intense. This is because we are always feeling our conditioned thinking in each moment.

The amazing insight is that a cycle of reactions is happening all the time to us, and we just have not been aware of it. Taking time to stop and reflect on our thinking gives us different insights around our reactions.

Let's explore what it means to be reactive versus responsive in more detail.

CHAPTER TWO
REACTIVE VERSUS RESPONSIVE

Reactive

The pace of life can get to everyone at times. As we mentioned earlier, when we are stressed, rushed, or distracted we operate in automatic pilot and in a state of **reaction**. Our vision is blurred as a result.

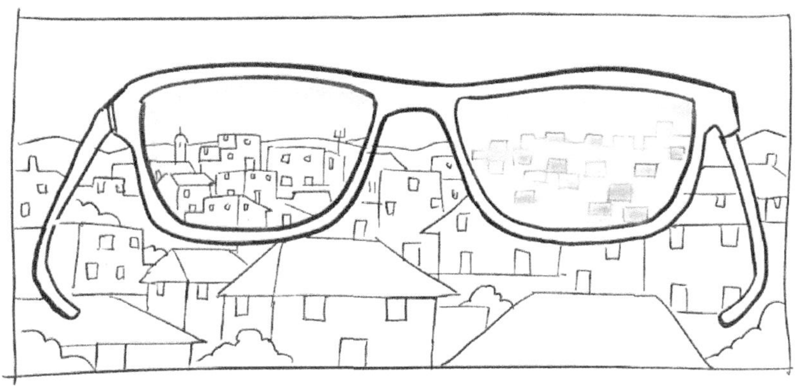

Something happens, we react.

Someone says something, we react.

Reaction is our conditioned response to something that we perceive **happens to us** in our day-to-day lives. Just like when you think, '***You***

make me so mad', 'I can't believe ***you hurt me*** like that', we believe that other people have the power to make us feel '_______(something)'.

Reacting happens automatically even when you're not thinking about it. This is because it's our socially and culturally conditioned human behaviour. You react based on how your emotions are triggered by your perception of the situation, which may be influenced by past experiences or other factors seemingly outside of your control.

Reacting is about letting your emotions and impulses take over without being aware of them.

This is when the ego hijacks emotions and puts them into a full range of actions to do anything to protect yourself. When we are in a mode of reacting, it often results in behaviour that's not consistent with your values or beliefs - which can have serious consequences for your mental health as well as your relationships with others. Being stuck in a state of reacting is very draining emotionally on a person and contributes to further feelings of being powerless to our circumstances.

Responsive

Our pre-frontal cortex is responsible for not only our motor tasks, but our judgement, abstract thinking, our creativity, and our thinking of what is socially appropriate. It is also responsible for emotions, our personality, self-control, muscle control and movement, and our memory storage.

As opposed to reacting, being **responsive** is a conscious choice of staying present in the moment to make space for reflection to consider a thoughtful response to any situation or trigger.

Something happens, we pause, we consider the event, we empathetically respond.

Someone says something, we pause, we consider their perspective, we curiously inquire further.

CQ Exercise:

Take a moment to ask yourself the question:

When a colleague said something in the workplace that you considered inappropriate for the situation, for example shouted at another colleague or customer, called someone a name, made a gesture, etc.

Did you react or respond to the event?

If so, what was the outcome?

If you choose to do this exercise, this is another appropriate time to use your journal to record your thinking and reflections. We quite often use a ***what, so what, now what*** reflection process. *What* was the situation / thought / event? *So what* does that mean to me / my team / my organisation / the situation experienced? and *Now what* does that mean I / we should do for me / my team / my organisation?

This process works well to explore thinking and reflect at a deeper level. Quite often the next step or action required reveals itself with great clarity. Misunderstandings become evident. Taking a curiosity stance can be very effective.

Dr. Jacqui finds another option to delve into an issue is asking several ***why's***? to get to the base of the reasoning or issue to then be able to address it.

This does remind us of our children when they were young and exploring the meaning of things and to understand. It quite often takes five why's to get to the root of the issue.

CQ Exercise:

Take a moment and reflect on your answers.

Write your thoughts down.

Then ask yourself:

If you reacted or responded - why did you react or respond that way?

Is there something you were unaware of that contributed to the situation?

Would you react or respond the same way next time?

Did you take any action? If so, why / why not?

What impact did that have on the dynamics of the relationship with the colleague?

What are you going to do about it?

Write your thoughts down.

Reflecting on your thoughts will give you different perspectives or lenses to consider. If you rushed in, the situation could become volatile quickly, creating a toxic situation to deal with. Considering the differing perspectives first, which can be quite quick, allows you to learn to be more responsive than reactive to future situations.

Disrupting our reactive mode

When we can disrupt our tendency to react to situations it is easy to see that the outcomes of being responsive are more productive. This is when you choose how you respond, based on what you can do and what your goals are. It is a conscious process of deciding how you want to behave in the moment. To be responsive requires awareness and presence *in* the moment, fully attentive to whatever you are experiencing.

When we are consciously aware and truly present in the moment to what is really happening, it is possible we can catch ourselves and snap out of being **reactive**. It is possible to disrupt the pattern and stop this ongoing cycle and shift to being **responsive**. We can consciously begin to point our awareness towards attentively conversing with others, actively listening to gaining collective input into decision making, and being creative when addressing misunderstandings.

The challenge then becomes how do we stay in a state of calm, the place where we can maintain being responsive?

Maintaining a responsive mode

This goes against the neuroscience of how our thinking system works since we are essentially geared up for crisis with our fight or flight response. When we feel stressed or anxious, our amygdala is triggered, as we mentioned earlier. What is known is that when this part of the brain is triggered, all other parts of the brain have a reduction in function so that all the energy and focus can be to protect us from the incoming threat. Makes sense.

As we relate this to our work environment, if most of the team are experiencing stress or anxiety, their amygdala is triggered, and they are in fight or flight mode. That means that the pre-frontal cortex part of the brain is temporarily reduced or dampened down so all the energy in the body can focus on getting ready to run from the threat, especially if their boss is perceived as a bear.

Why does this matter?

The pre-frontal cortex is the part of the brain where responsiveness lives, this is where your creativity comes from.

Now you can understand if your team is stressed or suffering anxiety, their creativity is **blocked** at a neurological level**.** Regardless of any fear-based tactics used by leaders to impose or threaten their teams. People cannot easily be creative or rational in this circumstance.

It is impossible to reason with anyone when they are in flight or fight mode. Have you tried this during a heated argument or when someone is shouting and angry. They are in full reaction mode; emotions have flared up and it is physically impossible to be sensible at that moment. It is impossible to listen to the other person or rationally consider the other person's perspective.

They need space to calm down.

Thinking Scenario
Rosa

Rosa had always been very shy and found it difficult to make friends with people at work. She found the learning about the balloon heads very helpful. She wrote down some of thinking she had about what her work colleagues might think about her:

- I've got nothing to say that's interesting.
- They aren't like me, so there's no point.
- I don't fit in with them.
- If they wanted to talk to me, they will have tried to.

Reading her notes gave Rosa the insight that her "balloon head" was filled with negative self-talk. It was clear that her thoughts were causing her to get stuck in some very negative conditioned thinking. Up until now, Rosa had just believed these thoughts without questioning them. She actually decided to share this in a session and to her surprise some other members of the team were very supportive and keen to do things differently.

They were open to connecting with her in a friendly way and that they didn't see her in the negative way that she feared they might. Of course, they each saw her through their own culturally conditioned lens, and guess what - their thoughts about her were a lot kinder than her thoughts about herself.

It is great when we take the opportunity to share things like this with a team. Many teams don't often get a chance to talk about such things to work colleagues in this way.

The team would all benefit from Rosa sharing her powerful insight about her "balloon head". Such authentic and honest discussions in an a psychologically safe space is needed. Cultural inQuiry™ created a new level of trust and connection between colleagues.

When we are calm, we can be open to the experiences and different perspectives. When we are relaxed and experiencing psychological safety, we can then begin to be creative. This is because the pre-frontal cortex, the part of our brain where creativity lives, is activated.

When reflecting on this, think about the reason why those great ideas pop into your head in the shower or when you are on a walk. Have you ever tried to remember something then whoosh, the answer arrives at 2am? This is because you are relaxed and there is new space for fresh thinking.

CQ Exercise:

Take a moment to ask yourself the question:

Have you ever had a great idea or fresh thinking pop into your head like this when you were relaxed?

It can be both frustrating and a great feeling, can't it?

The big question is, can we override our conditioned automatic reactions and replace them with clear sighted responsiveness?

The answer is: YES, of course, by learning how to integrate Cultural inQuiry to help improve your ability to connect with others. Our research confirms is that the majority of business issues are centred around the misperceptions that happen during human-to-human interaction[5].

This is the reason why **CQify**® was created, which means:

Cultural inQuiry, Insights For Yourself.

As you continue to read this book, you will discover that the real barriers to modern business and personal performance can be overcome with our new approach called: **CQify Cultural inQuiry™.**

Cultural **Inquiry**

CHAPTER THREE

CULTURAL INQUIRY™AND HOW IT IMPROVES OUR INNER AGILITY

Understanding Cultural inQuiry™

Cultural inQuiry™ is an opportunity to see the world with a fresh perspective. It is a chance to discover how cultural conditioning shapes our beliefs at an individual level. It is the progressive new way to reset organisational culture by overcoming any barrier that is preventing organisations from implementing their plans. By integrating insight-led communication, combined with our LENS Framework™, it is possible to co-create immediate measurable impact. By replacing old patterns with fresh ways to inspire creativity, your ***agility ability***™ can take your organisation to the next level.

Using Cultural inQuiry helps to co-create human-to-human connections.

Cultural inQuiry promotes a state of relentless curiosity when engaging with others to expand our awareness past our conditioned automatic assumptions to really know the person we are connecting with.

It is these human-to-human connections that generate the capacity of an organisation to deliver the results for customer, owners, stakeholders, and shareholders.

Use the QR code above to view our short corporate video that touches on the curiosity underpinning Cultural inQuiry™.

Glocalisation

Most people have heard of globalisation, but we are focusing on how glocalisation[1] (glo-cal-isation is what we all are currently experiencing, even if we are not yet aware of this. Actually, we are all citizens of the world or what we refer to as 'glocal' citizens. This means we are local to where we live, and we bring all our visible and invisible cultural identities with us, along with our local and global challenges we deal with every day.

PLEASE REMEMBER: This does not mean we don't honour, respect, value or forget the main or dominant culture to which we were born into or raised in. It just means now we have additional cultural influences that we have unconsciously personalised to our own unique way, the way we like it, the way that works for us in our lives.

Let us explain this further. For example, our friend was born in Spain. Her father was born in London, her mother was born in India and they both moved to Spain as young children. Our friend has been raised within a Spanish culture but has also been raised with English and Indian cultural traditions. As an adult she loves to celebrate the Spanish Fiestas (celebrations) and also integrates both English and Indian traditions into her life. So, it is impossible when you meet her to look at her to determine or assume where she was born, just like all of us.

When we meet new people in a glocalised world where migration is growing at a faster rate than the world population, it is good to remember this. Migration means people are moving around the world more than ever before in our history[28]. We are now working and living in different countries to where we were born and even to where our parents or grandparents were born[28]. The United Nations highlight that in 2019 there were 272 million migrations globally, an addition 51 million to 2010[28]. Organisations are and need to increasingly take a more glocal approach for their long-term sustainability as an organisation. Values and internal organisational cultures may change in the process.

Understanding this alone will change the conversation around connecting with others to co-creating an inclusive community, team, organisation, and world.

We begin to understand that it is impossible to attempt to apply historic cultural stereotypes to anyone. It is helpful that we meet people with the same level of open acceptance.

Case study: Dr. Kennedy, who wrote our forward, conducted Glocalisation research at a large multinational company to explore challenges being faced by the organisation developing culturally and linguistically appropriate web marketing content for its customers around the globe. He investigated conflicting perspectives around culture, linguistic and governance issues amongst those arguing for global one-size-fits-all perspectives to achieve cost efficiency and brand consistency, and those arguing for local perspectives that would deliver tailored web content for each market, content which could resonate with local customers and drive business locally. Dr. Kennedy looked for and found 'glocal' dynamics that could support achieving balance and harmony between the conflicting global and local perspectives. This required an understanding of the human-to-human interaction as outlined in this book. The use of glocal citizenship to better understand the differing perspectives allowed curiosity to seek out the best placement of content to the market and how people interact was effective. More is available on this case study (case study one) in the case study chapter at the rear of this book.

Using Cultural inQuiry, we greet each other with a refreshed openness to learn about the person and what different combinations of cultural traditions and customs they embrace. We can then effectively understand the impact of cultural influences on human behaviour and relationships.

It combines a deep reflection of how our individual cultural lens contributes to our worldview.

Cultural inQuiry unpacks our individuality so we can all be authentic and no longer be restricted by fear, our social masks, or our egos. We can shift our perspectives through the realisation that we all are having separate realities and there are many different ways of seeing the world.

This conscious process of making the invisible visible is possible when we are open to include multiple perspectives to help us see what we don't see.

Dr. Cari's research[5] shows that when we iterate multiple perspectives into the decision making process, it is not only more robust, but also easier to implement with reduced resistance.

Everything we do and say is always filtered through another person's lens, blurred by whatever they are going through at the moment.
They can only see themselves.
So, however they see you, is really only about them.

Dr. Cari

CQify ® Is Changing Minds

Let's explore this concept further. In making the invisible, visible, we consider differing perspectives, drawing on the experiences we each bring to the discussion. In embracing the unique CQify® approach, we are experiencing how Cultural inQuiry™ is increasing engagement, and how this is changing minds in the process. Participants creating space for several differing insights that have become game-changers for them and their organisation.

Dr. Cari shares that last year when speaking to CEOs of multinational companies at a conference, one came up after the presentation to say he never even realised the team has been stuck in the reaction mode of automatic pilot when it came to management. The insight experienced was understanding why the team has not been performing to their normal standard. It was because of the misunderstandings causing arguments, missing deadlines, calling in sick, quitting and so on. The manager would react to a colleague who would further react to another, and no collaboration could occur. Once the CEO learned about this cycle of reaction it was possible to understand what was needed to shift the organisational culture. He realised why nothing was improving, regardless of the new technology implemented or the new training sessions or processes that were undertaken. Now with CQify he could tackle the real issue.

Dr. Jacqui has had a similar experience but at a staff level. In an organisation where she was consulting, staff were so focused on the business as usual they were on a continual cycle of automatic pilot and missed opportunities to not only develop themselves but advance the organisation towards the agreed vision. They were blind to what was happening around them, cocooning themselves in creating no time for any reflection or insights to emerge, and losing customers in the process. Complaints were responded to with reference to being too busy, it was someone else's problem or issue, and customers were being too demanding. Yet, individually, each believed they were being a team player and customer-centric in their focus. It wasn't until a reflective mirror exercise was put up to the staff members that greater understanding of their self-sabotaging was happening to the level of challenging their ongoing roles. It became their respective 'ah ha' moment, their understanding of how their reaction mode was creating the challenges they faced (further information is available in case study two in the case study chapter).

These examples highlight the reactive versus responsive thinking in play. In this case, the following image shows the responsive clear lens versus the reactive unfocused lens.

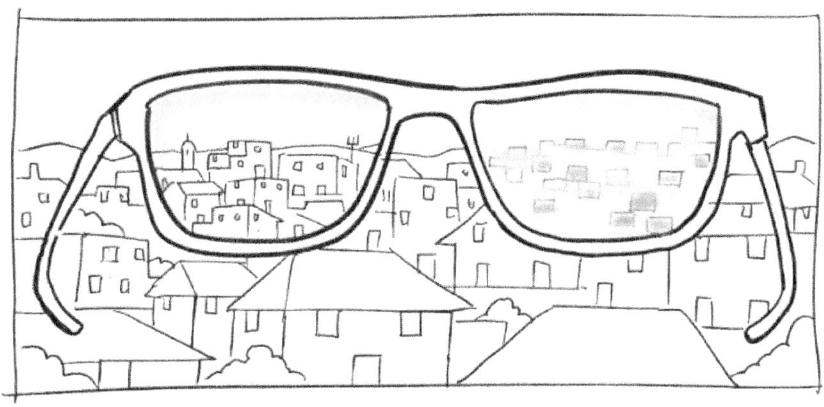

The bottom line is that many business challenges are due to interpersonal conflict and misunderstandings which happen based on different perceptions that occur during any human-to-human interaction.

We can unlearn to learn from each other and be open to see the world from a different perspective, which we discuss more in the next section.

CHAPTER FOUR
UNLEARN TO LEARN

We don't know
what we don't know
until we know it

Unlearning

Unlearning is such a valuable concept that many people struggle with, especially when it comes to personal beliefs, social and cultural conditioning. We often hold on to our views of the world and ourselves because they are familiar, they become habits and patterns even if they are no longer working for us. Our unquestioned information that we have collected over our lifetime is part of our unconscious bias that informs our everyday decision making. This is what is used to create our personal perception of reality.

Unlearning can be difficult because, in most cases, we often have an emotional attachment to our beliefs, ideas, and identities. Sometimes we hold on to things that no longer serve us because we fear change; other times we cling to them because they give us a sense of identity or belonging. Unlearning requires our willingness to let go of what we've known before and may be uncomfortable in the process of finding something new. It can feel risky or scary. On the other hand, the freedom of taking this step leads to new possibilities of experiencing life in a better way that you never could have imagined.

This chapter explores why some people perceive that it is difficult to unlearn or challenge their beliefs about themselves as well as their judgements about others or society.

The intention is to invite you to explore this journey as a process that assists each of us to review, renew and let go of old patterns, habits, and beliefs for deep personal growth.

This does not mean that you must forget your past, but rather, learn and reflect on life lessons to potentially source or apply new information as required. Self-reflection is the key to achieving deep relationships with others and to develop your **inner ability agility** by inviting all perspectives without judgement.

Dr. Cari considers it all begins with awareness. In her research, she found that 85% of research participants did not know they had unconscious bias or realise the impact their culture had on their existing beliefs and behaviours[5].

Self-reflection

We both personally and professionally integrate self-reflection in all aspects of our decision making and relationship building. Reflecting on our perceptions of how a situation went and asking:

- Did I fully understand the person or the situation?
- What internal dialogue was disrupting the conversation? and
- What could have gone better?

This is so helpful when we are nurturing connections with others. We are always aware of just how easy it is for misunderstandings to happen when we are busy and simply not paying attention. As we blurt out a conversation without concentrating or even making sure the other person heard what we meant to say, then there is a high possibility of a misunderstanding that we are not even aware of. This is when people in your life just stop calling you, or you get ghosted. We are sure you can relate to this or something similar that happened in your life or to someone you know.

What we know for sure is that when people make the space to deeply reflect on lessons learned in the moment, it can fuel our passion to learn more in order to break through toxic patterns or habits. To do so, we must commit to being open to always learning. Become life-long learners.

Sometimes it is possible that we keep doing the same things or the same patterns unconsciously that hinder our connections with others. It can change immediately with awareness and reflection. We have the power to stop our own cycle of suffering and deeply connect with ourselves and others. We think this is important to know.

Impact of change through self-reflection

Dr. Cari shares that we can see the freedom people experience when they leave a bad job, relationship or situation and realise their true passions. We have seen a lawyer quit his job and become a teacher. His parents wanted him to follow in the family footsteps as they were all lawyers, but his deep passion was to help young people. We can see people shift their behaviours and beliefs after a personal trauma such as a loss of their job, a loss of a colleague or family member, a divorce or illness, any of which can jolt us into opening up to new ideas, concepts, or opportunities that we never considered before.

Embracing the choice to unlearn

The concept of unlearning any of our personal beliefs and social conditioning is actually not a difficult one. When trying the process, it does surprise people just how easy it is.

It can be done with awareness - and it's worth doing.

It's easy to get stuck in a cycle of believing whatever we were taught to believe as children, or what we were taught and absorbed from the people around us when we were young. In fact, we are constantly fuelling up our perceptions by gathering information from our surroundings and other people all the time. We are unaware of what is going in our subconscious programming.

It's hard to see that it is possible that some beliefs we have acquired in our lifetime from others, or our environment may not work for us personally, but we do have choice. Our research confirms that everyone can shift their thinking easily and be free to experience what we choose for ourselves.

There are many benefits to **un**learning some of our personal beliefs and social conditioning. These include:

1. We are able to see things from new perspectives, which allows us to make better choices in life and work.
2. We are able to show more humility when we identify what our own biases are so we can shift them if we want to.
3. We become more compassionate towards others, because we are able to see things from their point of view.
4. We can experience deep connections with others to overcome misunderstandings so we can collaborate easily to implement our plans.

The changing guard of management styles

When we think of a traditional view of working, Dr. Cari, based on her research[5], explains that most people have experienced a demanding boss that manages others through fear-based thinking, by shouting, threatening, and intimidating their team members to achieve identified Key Performance Indicators (KPI's)[2] or other performance markers.

This style of leadership is no longer tolerable in today's hyper competitive and hybrid world that now requires more autonomy and self-regulation. People are looking for a business role that also enables them to contribute to society with purpose and passion that offers a psychologically safe space to contribute. We want to feel good about what we do for a living, how we are taking care of ourselves, others, and the planet. We want to be part of an ethical purpose that nurtures our personal growth and helps a greater cause.

Dr. Jacqui agrees. Rather than being the investigator of bullying and harassment claims, it was a very different feeling having been on the receiving end of an over demanding manager. Upon reflection, it was actually bullying rather than a command-and-control management style, that created a psychologically unsafe environment. Although such an environment should not exist, it does, and it's an environment that can't continue long-term for our mental health and organisational productivity.

On further reflection, Dr. Jacqui gained insights from the experience to understand that perhaps the bullying behaviour of the manager was out of fear of not performing herself or feeling less adequate than her staff for whatever reason. Unfortunately, this leader lost a number of good quality staff as a result of her approach to 'management'. From subsequent observation, it is still clear she has not realised bullying does not work.

> It is the disruptive and unproductive management cycles that individuals need to unlearn to learn new patterns that are productive and offer a psychologically safe work environment for their staff. In doing so, staff satisfaction, retention and productivity rises.[6,10,11]
>
> *Dr. Jacqui*

While reviewing the current working environment with all the different training, technology or business solutions offered, we understand how this can be confusing. Even though previous approaches have been valuable in the past, present challenges now require a radically fresh idea. Clearly, unlearning needs to happen for new insights to occur.

This is a powerful example of why **UNLEARNING** needs to happen.

It is time to be open to integrate new knowledge that will better inform today's organisational needs, based on the changing landscape of human interaction, glocalisation, migration and technology. We think that this realisation helps makes sense around the current confusion about how to manage people effectively, how to co-create high performing teams or navigate the complexity of co-creating value within an organisation.

This confusion also extends into what style of leadership will help resolve the above challenges. We have seen continuous attempts and multiple efforts to identify a form or style of leadership that can be all encompassing for every situation, which we can confirm does not exist. Especially with the new modern challenges such as non-linear decision making and knowledge sharing combined with ongoing uncertainty and complexity.

From our perspective, there is no single formula to lead in this environment.

If any one specific style of leadership and management worked, we would not have such a high failure rate for organisational growth, performance, and lack of employee satisfaction.

This became very thought provoking as we explored this challenge on a deeper level.

What we are experiencing is that traditional leadership needs to be upskilled for today's new way of working. There are many examples we can share from both our practical experience and research. With remote teams, people need to be prepared to balance autonomy with accountability. There also needs to be a new space for the insights to flow as a co-creator of high performing teams. Without this foundation of knowledge, organisations are being held back by people who are resisting all forms of change, with people that we describe as a form of behaviour associated with 'Blocking'.

Let's deep dive into this further in the next chapter.

CHAPTER FIVE
UNBLOCKING THE BLOCKER

The blocker

When we are not in the **flow of Cultural inQuiry**™, it is easy to slip back to old patterns. This is a significant challenge for the leadership team when there is a person(s) in the organisation whose behaviour is considered to be a ***blocker***.

Achieving the ultimate organisational flow means that all members are seamlessly in a state of syncronised creativity and collaboration. The foundation of achieving this level of psychological safety requires responsive team communication. It can be challenging to shift towards a co-creative flow without first recognising the barriers.

The person or people we refer to as displaying behaviour as a 'blocker(s)' is a real barrier to a healthy culture and organisational performance. What is interesting from our perspective is that at some point, we can potentially relate to innocently being a blocker ourselves on ocassion.

Dr. Cari has experienced the CEO saying: 'yes let's proceed with the proposal, just meet with my executives to discuss the implementation'. Sounds simple, right? Absolutely not! Many executive teams, but not all, include someone who is a ***blocker.*** This is the person that is respected enough by the CEO that they follow their recommendations at face value without digging deeper into the potential reasons the blocker is sabotaging or rejecting their decisions. This person can be the CEO's greatest blind spot if left unchecked. The blocker is the person who is feeling the most threatened by any new approach, concept, or idea, albeit subconsciously.

It is very common for the blocker to use all sorts of different behaviours, like manipulation and fear-based tactics, to protect their desired control over others or the situation. When we describe a blocker, we consider it would be someone who repeatedly shows up as the person who has been there, done that, or says 'oh yes, we have done this before and it didn't work', or is ready to bridge their lack of knowledge with excuses on why the decision or initiative should not proceed. If you recall earlier, we also shared about how our egos can flare up, which could also contribute to blocker behaviour.

Additionally, the blocker is normally guided by reacting to situations. Being more ego-led, the blocker has a personal agenda, and is threatened by the risk of being wrong, losing power or influence. A blocker, or a person resisting any different perspectives or learning opportunities, is a hazard to all initiatives to enhance high performing teams. This person has a blurred view of reality that can only be seen with their blinkers on. We are sure you will have come across a person like this before. You may also, on reflection, realise you have even been that person at times.

Fear-based thinking is the navigating force at work in ***blockers*** and ego-led management reactions.

What do we mean by fear-based thinking?

Fear-based thinking

This is when our fears trigger and dominate our thinking patterns. As we mentioned earlier, fear could be from never feeling good enough, or just being wrong.

Could it be that some business leaders are still wrapping decision making, corporate strategy and culture in the traditional comfort blankets? Yet, they are still neglecting the need to unwrap the toxic baggage that cocoons egos and blocks true human-to-human connection.

In our view, this is another extreme example of a blocker, which is exhibiting a level of toxic behaviour based on their perceived power, level of self-importance, and being ego-led. Regardless of the others in the organisation, their individual actions are actually sabotaging the company's performance.

Case study: An example of such blocking, drawing from case study three in the case study chapter, we know a group of company directors that are interested in selling their company. Although there have been a few key investors looking to buy this company, it has never sold. The potential reason from our perspective is simple: there are no collective leadership initiatives being rolled out due to the lack of respect between the directors, which is resulting in a high level of incompetency and toxicity throughout the organisation.

During the due diligence process when potential purchasers start analysing the company processes and people, it is impossible to hide a toxic work culture. The blind spot is that each director believes it's the other one's fault, and blame will not change any outcomes.

When there is solely an ego-led style of leadership, some of the common symptoms exhibited are that they are never wrong, apathy towards key people quitting, board room bullying, and no desire for personal or professional development. There is a blind belief that they are the best and who cares about the rest. Sound familiar?

When there is no space for reflection, no openness to unlearn, and no curiosity or consideration of other perspectives, the toxic cycle will continue and eventually implode.

In our experience, the lone rangers that ride off to do as they please block everyone's **agility ability**™, which inevitably results in an undercurrent of dissatisfied employees and clients. It is not surprising that every potential buyer has always walked away from the business in case study three after due diligence and experiencing the toxic relationships.

The key outcome is that even though the business is viable and creating profit due to the niche market it is in, no purchaser wants to take on this toxic organisational culture. The blind spot is that the company directors don't even realise this and believe in the blame game, that it is someone else's fault. Sadly, this is a common business case.

We are sharing this business case because it is a great example of how organisations can get and remain stuck. This is an ongoing toxic cycle of denial, intimidation and fear-based decision making or thinking. Another potential perspective could be they are threatened to even begin to acknowledge the problem, because if they do, it becomes real. In the meantime, the suffering continues and is affecting all levels of relationships with key staff and customers.

Removing the blinkers ...and blockers

CQ Dr. Cari has experienced conversations with CEOs that are blind to how the division heads within their companies are actually blockers or barriers to performance. There is one specific case where the executives meet every two months to discuss strategy, they agree on action points and go back to their allocated roles/divisions. Then one of the executive leaders just continues managing his division his own way and fails to respect or implement the agreed plans from the meetings.

How do you think this affects the overall performance of the organisation? How would you respond if this was happening within your executive team? What type of consequences should be put in place?

In our role as a **CQify Critical Friend**®, we would encourage reflection on the opportunity costs of the leadership team's actions. This would also be the same for the directors trying to sell their organisation. These challenges can begin to shift simply with a willingness to be aware of their own conditioned thinking and different perspectives that may have not been previously considered. The recommended approach is to explore what the real invisible consequence of this behaviour is having on the team or people under this direct leadership. Then consider what the leadership team's toxic relationships with each other are modelling to the rest of the team.

Can you imagine what it would be like to show up for work in either of these types of environments?

The common reaction is to dismiss this type of person or people if they are not willing to shift their behaviours or even leave the company yourself. The good news is that there is a mid-way option to resolve and reset situations, just like the two shared above, by embedding **CQify's Cultural inQuiry**™.

Pioneering change

CQ Cultural inQuiry is pioneering change on this front by showing that even **blockers and ego-led leaders or managers** can shift their behaviour by becoming curious about their innocent misunderstandings of perceived threats, insecurities, and misuse of power. Dr. Cari has seen first-hand the boardroom bully completely shift their toxic behaviours with the new understanding about how our minds work.

When you are in the flow of Cultural inQuiry, you see the innocence of the blocker. It is now possible to see that they are experiencing an innocent misunderstanding which can explain their behaviour because they are coming from fear-based thinking. It is almost like magic, once we are aware of our fear-based thinking, we realise it is possible for everyone, even the blocker to have a new experience.

With this fresh perspective, we understand that all existing knowledge can now be helpful once the blocker has an insight into their own behaviour. This shift enables them to be a co-creator and contributor that is no longer blocking progress but showcasing their ability to be agile, their agility ability™.

When you begin to embed Cultural inQuiry within your organisation, you will find the balloon thinking is reduced so you can see each other's faces again, including the bully and anyone previously filled with 'hot air'.

Now, on the one hand, we do need people on the leadership team and throughout the organisation that are willing to stand up against the status quo and challenge the thinking of others. What if, on the other hand, co-creators are already doing that intrinsically as part of participating in a high performing team. We have been able to see how powerful this shift in perspective is.

The difference that we share is that instead of silently encouraging a 'blocker' style behaviour, we pivot to seek out people that can be our **'CQify C*ritical Friend*'**®.

But what is a CQify Critical Friend you ask?

CQ Critical **Friend**

CQify Critical Friend®

A CQify Critical Friend is an expert or a group of international experts that can gently challenge the thinking of a CEO and leadership teams in a non-threatening positive way. This process can provide instant access to evidence-based insights that can be directly applied to the issue being faced. This unbiased conversation can be very helpful, especially for decisions that need urgent attention with no time for extensive research.

Many people perceive the term ***critical*** as being difficult, or even outright mean.

We are using the word 'critical' to describe a way to challenge the existing norms, the status quo, and to initiate a deeper conversation with multiple perspectives to make robust decisions that have minimal bias and no hidden agendas. Just clarity, transparency, and truth.

Have you ever considered what lost opportunities are missed due to leadership blind spots?

What are the lost opportunities when a board or team suffers from 'group think'? Group think is when people go along with the consensus or what the boss says, for fear of disrupting the status quo or being wrong. Also known as a 'yes person', always answering 'yes', no matter the issue, decision or action recommended.

A ***CQify Critical Friend*** can help decision makers consider the issue from different perspectives and reflect on their own. This type of progressive executive team is built on the dynamics of valuing all perspectives, and who are willing to participate and have their thinking challenged in a critical friendly way. This is a missing link in most organisations, and leadership teams can often miss opportunities due to prolonged decision-making processes or that do not consider multiple perspectives. Having your thinking and decisions challenged is a progressive way forward to robust actions and accountability.

Imagine if you could contact a **critical friend** to bounce ideas off, tap immediately into multiple perspectives that are supported by up-to-date research to help inform your decisions and reflect individually. How would this change **yourself, your team, your organisation, and your** world?

Utilising a critical friend on demand can help us to begin to acknowledge our reactive thinking versus our responsive thinking. It is an offering that CQify has, where CEOs and executives can tap into an independent **critical friend**® to bounce ideas around, check thinking, seek out research and best practices, and offer a reflective sounding board.

A critical friend is not a mentor or a coach, but more of a mirror to help you as a leader reflect on the invisible barriers and to help make them visible while pointing out significant insights generated. How to recognise and acknowledge our reactive thinking and shift towards being responsive in the moment is a powerful foundation for co-creativity and developing your agility ability™.

Another advantage of using a critical friend is while we are relaxed and reflective about our thinking it is possible for insights to appear. Insights are the foundations or the engine of innovation. In this next section we will share more.

CHAPTER SIX
PRESCRIPTIVE TECHNIQUES vs INSIGHT-LED COMMUNICATION

How we view the world

The core issue we are discussing goes beyond just making plans or putting them into action. It really starts with how each person views things, people, or their world, while recognising that the benefit to the team is that we all think differently. This is the way we can work together to really achieve our goal and stay on track, regardless of what urgent situation we are facing at that moment.

Imagine that nothing can take you off track and you are always fearlessly surfing change. Not drowning in it.

It is only when we are in a state of mind that is calm, when we are relaxed, or not feeling threatened that we can be creative and experience connection with others.

Co-creating is about sharing our challenges with others so we can generate new insights together. Insights are new ideas that evolve within us when we are inspired, calm and psychologically safe. We can be accountable for our own views and why we perceive things a certain way to appreciate the value other perspectives can bring to the conversation. The foundation of this type of interaction is all based upon sharing mutual respect.

This is how insight-led learning and communication happens and advances the traditional way of applying prescriptive techniques. Let us explain further.

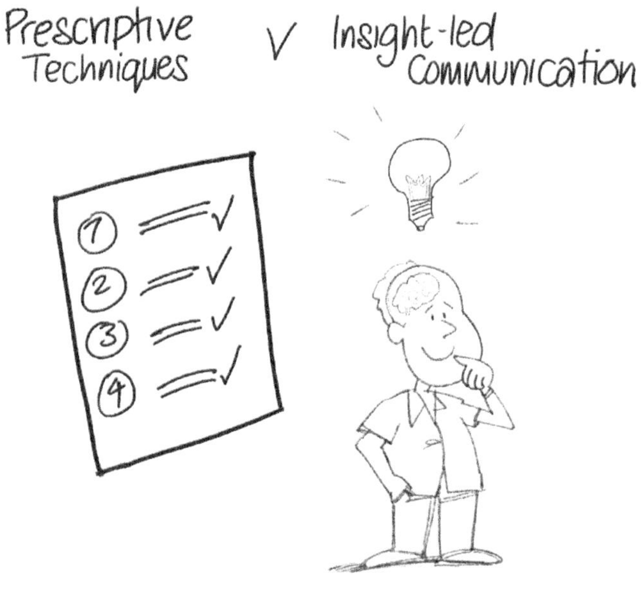

Prescriptive techniques

Prescriptive techniques are based on traditional training methods and thinking. Examples are when you receive specific instructions to follow, like apply the following three steps or this specific tool will solve your problem. An interesting observation is that these techniques are normally put ON TO people or they are forced to follow, which can also trigger various forms of resistance.

Some examples of prescriptive techniques are: The three ways to improve your sales pitch, the six steps to effective communication, or the five things to do for successful leadership, and so on. The main issue is that the prescriptive techniques do not go deep enough to disrupt our automatic pilot. They neglect the principles of neuroscience, where resilience psychology about how to get to the core of shifting the human experience. Another issue is the ambiguity of the steps, due to the various perceptions and needs people have that we will expand on further along.

Prescriptive training techniques are very valuable in some circumstances, such as when you need to follow a safety protocol for medical professionals, plumbing or electrical work. There will be a specific set of steps required to complete a task or action. This is where we need to follow exact instructions or face consequences. For example, like a fire hazard if steps are missed as an electrician, or your house gets flooded because of a mistake the plumber made.

Once we have memorised the instructions there is no further need to think or even discover other ideas outside of those rules. We become unconsciously competent. It becomes second nature as an automatic process.

But what happens when a new policy is developed, or a new tool comes on the market to make our jobs easier?

This disruption to our routine and existing knowledge can cause our balloon head to inflate with our stress. For example, we are required to adapt to new policies announced to the company to be sure everyone is aware of them and know to follow them without question. For some, this is quite acceptable and they are compliant. For others, it creates stress through change, needing to follow a new process, fear of making an error, and so on.

Do you buy the new tool to make your job more efficient and easier or do you stick with the tool you have always used? The one that you are comfortable with? The one you know is tried and tested that you trust? How do you feel when you see a completely new tool versus an improved traditional one? Most people would choose the improved traditional tool as it is something they are familiar with. Interesting how human nature prevails and is embedded within us.

When we are on a team and there is a constant flow of change, a constant influx of new tools to choose from, we can become overwhelmed, sceptical, fearful, and unsure which one to use, what one is best. It could be perceived as easier at this point to have someone just tell us what to do. Or is it that on some level we even expect or want somebody to tell us what to do and how to navigate uncertainty, so we don't make the wrong decision. Then we don't need to be accountable if something goes wrong and we don't need to even think, we can just follow. This is obviously the easier choice to make even though it can be considered a more passive option.

What if we are the leader, how do we make an educated decision about what to do next to overcome the issues at hand? What if we make the wrong decision? How do we look as leaders? What other pressures and fears do we face as leaders of the organisation?

When we look at all the different versions of reality it is much easier to understand the foundation of fear-based thinking that exists on all levels of the organisation.

This is exactly the reason why organisations are getting stuck.

Insight-led communication

If we revisit this:

What happens if we can replace fear-based thinking with fresh new insights? What if there are no limiting boundaries, protocols, KPI's, or threats preventing us from being our best creative selves? What if there is no pressure?

This is the advantage of insight-based learning and communication that inspires everyone's voice and contribution. Insights are sights from within us, new acknowledged thoughts that happen in our creative flow. When we see something for ourselves, without being told, there is a higher possibility we will apply it to our life, and work. When **me** turns to **we,** it is possible for us to co-create new ideas in a psychologically safe ecosystem, where our ability to become more agile, our **agility ability**™ is unlimited.

Thinking Scenario
Jeremiah

Jeremiah enjoyed his role as a CEO of a small start-up, but he was finding it difficult to deal with a challenging colleague. The colleague often complained when given tasks to do. Jeremiah saw Jon as someone who was negative and needed to be micro-managed...

Jeremiah realised that he felt anxious even before he spoke to Jon about something. He always tried to get in first and say what he needed to say quickly to get the meeting over with. Jeremiah had the insight that he didn't need to do that at all anymore. He had the insight that his job as CEO was also to build an agile team, rather than just fire orders at everyone and "fix" their problems.

So, Jeremiah decided he would schedule a block of time to really listen to Jon's concerns about the project they were working on. Jeremiah told Jon that he wanted to hear how he felt things were going. It was interesting because as he listened to Jon deeply (as he had been taught to in Cultural inQuiry sessions) he saw how anxious and worried Jon really was. This gave him some compassion for Jon. Jeremiah hadn't realised that Jon was so committed to getting things "right" for the client. He had an insight that "Jon doesn't think he is being moaning, he thinks he is pointing out problems that have to be fixed!" This is separate realities at play.

Jeremiah had been conditioned to identify problems to be the fixer and offer solutions. He welcomes the idea that "We could do this differently...." He also realised how he labelled Jon as difficult and moaning. Those labels are just one way of thinking about Jon. Jeremiah saw instinctively that Jon is so much more than just those labels he had given him, and it didn't help either of them when Jeremiah saw him from that biased perspective.

Jeremiah also saw how he rushed in to fix problems Jon identified. This time he offered Jon the chance to talk about how he might tackle the problems he himself had identified. This involved meeting several times. Jeremiah deliberately gave Jon space to answer his own questions in advance and then share his answers with Jeremiah in a subsequent meeting. It felt like they were really co-creating a response to the issues Jon raised, and in honesty, some of Jon's ideas were good. Jeremiah had the insight that Jon was able to identify solutions to the problems he presented when he was given the time and space to do so. It turns out that Jon just needed to be heard.

From this point on Jeremiah reminded Jon in each meeting that he trusted his knowledge about the client and would like the team to hear some more of his solutions to tackle the problems that he identified in the next meeting. They scheduled another meeting for the following week and Jon presented his concerns and some possible solutions for discussion with the rest of the team. In this way the co-creating team had just got bigger.

This is the first time Jeremiah had seen the possibility of turning "Me into We". To be honest it was a relief for him to feel that he was not the only one who could look at the problem from a different angle.

Dr. Cari's research[5] confirms, and we have further substantiated, that when an organisation's culture is focused on co-creating a psychologically safe ecosystem, creativity flows and is enhanced. The **me** becomes **we**.

Now that we understand the psychological and neurological processes that occur, and we are aware of how to disrupt the cycle of reactivity to being more responsive. The next aspect to deconstruct is to consider the difference between our state of mind, versus our mindset in more detail.

CHAPTER SEVEN
STATE OF MIND VERSUS MINDSET

Mindset

Mindset training has been happening for decades and has been positive in gaining interest and awareness about how we think. There are many different success stories about how it has helped people to connect how their thinking can influence their behaviours.

This initiative has seen increasing popularity and is focused on changing our mindset. We are sure you have heard about how to create a growth mindset or positive mindset? If not, for the purpose of clarity, our definition is that our mindset determines how we interpret and react to certain situations, based on our perceptions, beliefs, feelings, and attitudes.

For example, traditionally if you wanted to change your current mindset to having a growth mindset, it means you want to change the way you think and react in your personal reality. First, we would like to highlight the importance of acknowledging that your current abilities or skills are not something that are fixed and unchanging. Instead, it's about understanding that you can always improve yourself if you so wish. It is OK to accept that the risk of failure is just part of the process. A growth mindset is the belief that your abilities, intelligence, and talents can be developed through dedication and hard work. This means that when you have a growth mindset, you don't see mistakes as failures - you see them as opportunities to learn something new.

When we consider that the opposite of a growth mindset is a fixed one, we can understand that these people believe in fixed traits. For example, that their abilities are set in stone and can't change over time or with effort. A lot of time we can observe that the person we referred to earlier as a 'blocker' possesses these traits. A fixed mindset person may say things like: 'I am who I am' or 'this is how I was raised' or 'I was only taught this way' or 'I don't know any other way'.

As times are changing with new circumstances, people's needs are also changing. During our research we discovered we are actually dynamic beings. Meaning that we are always experiencing different states of mind that are changing constantly in every moment. We are not static in our thinking or how we are experiencing life.

It was quite thought provoking to realise that regardless of our chosen mindset, we are still experiencing a full range of emotions. The challenge is that different emotions may not fit with your desired mindset.

The good news is that it is unrealistic to believe we can achieve and remain in one static mindset. This is not even desirable or possible from a neurological perspective.

We have both attended many different mindset training sessions over the years. We get all fired up and motivated to change our mindsets. We have all the steps we need to implement in our lives, but a few weeks later we return back to our normal habits and routines. Has this ever happened to you? Have you ever been excited about a new way of doing something only to see it fizzle out quickly and wonder why our pre-programmed habits always seem to win? We have also been curious to learn why this happens, regardless of the quality of the trainer or speaker ......it appears to us that human nature prevails.

Then it hit us, it's all in the name: Mind **SET.**

We know from our previous discussion in the past sections that our minds never permanently **SET**, our minds are always wondering, our moods are always changing moment to moment, which influences our attitudes and actions.

Then we began to observe the mental chatter that would start within us. We started to be hard on ourselves for not being able to maintain a positive mind SET, or a growth mind SET or whatever the latest mind SET is trending at the moment.

Then we noticed how this put us in a negative mind SET wondering why others could maintain it but not us. Although, when we begin to reflect on mind SET it is easy to see how something SET can never be useful in today's dynamic and complex daily life. It's time to advance the concept of mind SET to something that can help us navigate ongoing complexity and uncertainty.

We started to shift our focus about our:

CURRENT STATE OF MIND.......

This was a real game changer.

State of mind

Let's explain. We can invite you to imagine an elevator that has 10 floors which start in the basement and goes up to the upper floor.

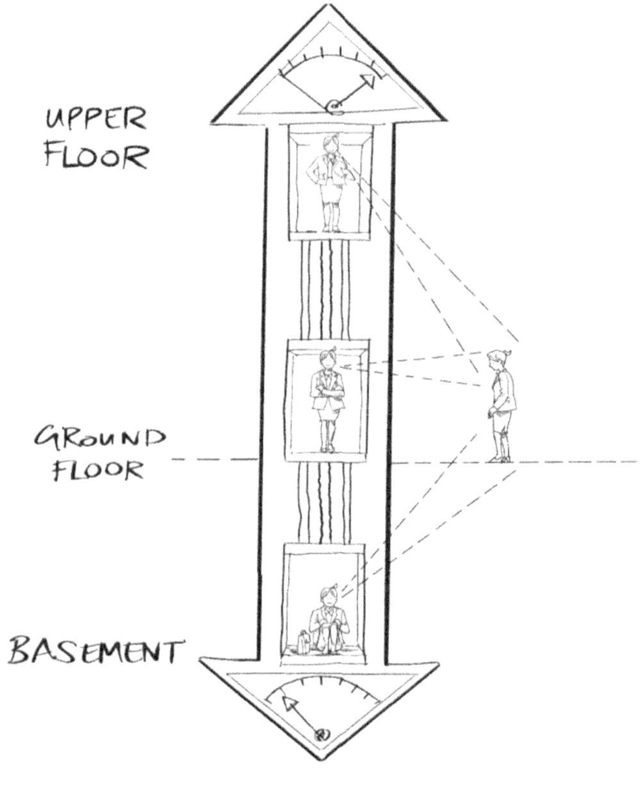

Remembering that we are all balloon heads. From the moment we wake up and the alarm goes off, our mind floods with thoughts about our list of things to do. We can already start to feel stressed, putting our state of mind at floor level 1. Then we remember our boss is taking the team out to our favourite restaurant for lunch today, so our state of mind goes up to level 8. In the next moment as we are on our way into the office there is a roadblock, so we are going to be late. What!?? YIKES if we are late, we could get fired .....if we get fired, we will lose our house, if we lose our house, we will have nowhere to live ....so our elevator slams into the basement. Then to our surprise the roadblock clears, and we are back on our way. Arriving only a few minutes late, our boss calls us to his office and offers us a raise for all our hard work ...whoosh our elevator is on the upper floor!

I am sure you get the idea now on how we are all influenced minute by minute with our state of mind.

Now in the context of how we connect with others it is much easier to understand that if we are 'balloon heads'© with our current state of mind elevator going up and down all the time, imagine just how difficult it is to apply a specific leadership or communication style to ourselves and others. The important thing to stress here is that it is our thinking in the moment that is causing the elevator to go up and down. We don't need to change our thinking - just acknowledge that we are thinking and what floor we are on in that moment. When we reflect deeper, we can learn that depending on what floor we are at will influence our perspective and view.

For example, if you are on the upper floor when you look to people on the main level you will only see the top of their heads. Then of course if you are in the basement with your current state of mind when you look up to the main floor you will only see the bottom of everyone's shoes. This is symbolic of how your current state of mind can influence your perspective about life in the moment.

Knowing that our elevator (or lift) is moving up and down, helps explain why when our thinking changes our perspectives change and so do our feelings and therefore our moods. This means if you are in the basement at the moment, it doesn't mean that you will be there forever. Afterall, neuroplasticity has proved that we have the capacity to have fresh new thinking in the moment. As we said before, when the mind is calm, we can have fresh insights more easily.

Then we can begin to realise that we are all feeling our thinking in every moment, we are dynamic, not static beings, which is a real eye opener why prescriptive training initiatives do not provide a long-term shift in our capabilities. It is easier to understand that if your team is having basement thinking, now won't be the best time to do a brainstorming session.

For example, in our office before a meeting starts, we always check in with everyone to see where their elevator is at. Sometimes that is all it takes to lift an elevator from basement thinking to floor 5, sometimes we need to do more to support each other and other times we have rescheduled meetings. There are no rules, no KPI's, no micromanaging, just accountability, acknowledgment, and acceptance of where we really are at that moment.

As a thriving company we know that this helps to really connect in the moment and achieve whatever task is in focus. On the other hand, we have had leaders share that they would be concerned the meeting would turn into counselling sessions, be a time waster, or take away from the true purpose of the meeting. That is an example of fear-based thinking. We are not recommending an in-depth analysis into someone's current state of mind but merely naming what is not visible, so we can take our 'current state of mind' into account.

In our experience, it opens the conversation up so people can bring their whole selves to work, be seen, be heard and collaborate. Knowing we are all balloon heads, with varying levels of stress, anxiety, worry, joy, peace, and happiness can be helpful. It also improves are ability to understanding each other and taking out the assumptions, guess work and judgement of what is going on with one another.

Thinking Scenario
Frederich

Frederich found the state of mind elevator diagram very helpful. A lot of his job was about listening to others talking about their problems and trying to find solutions for them. Sometimes he would get home from work and was exhausted from listening to others. He was starting to think he was close to "burnout" and considering resignation.

Frederich had an insight that he was taking his thinking from work home with him and spending fruitless hours replaying the conversations he had in work in his mind. He saw, insightfully, that it was repetitive thinking that was exhausting him. He loved the idea that "you can't trust all your thinking when you are in the basement."

He had the insight that his self-compassion and common sense went out the window when he was "in the basement" because of the "flight, fright, freeze response."

It turns out that when we have less thinking on our mind and really understand our feeling is coming from our thinking, our state of mind elevator can begin to rise naturally again.

Achieving psychological safety for the individuals on your team is a top priority for leaders as people cannot thrive and be creative without it. Indeed, lack of such psychological safety is one of the main reasons for people quitting and reduced innovation. But we first need to consider that the basis of any misunderstanding begins with ourselves and our own perceptions of the world.

The human mind is a powerful thing. It can be used to shape our lives in ways that are both constructive and destructive. In many cases, we are our own worst enemy.

We can wholeheartedly relate to this.

It can be surprising to realise that we automatically allow our thoughts to control us and dictate our actions or re-actions. Our thoughts are often just illusions or false mental concepts that we have created for ourselves. They do not always represent reality or truth. They are often simply ideas that we have conjured up in our minds, based on past experiences and external factors such as advertising campaigns, media, or other people's opinions. In this sense our thoughts are culturally conditioned.

We do not have to believe everything we think, see, or hear. In fact, it would be helpful not to. Cultural inQuiry allows us to be far more discerning about which thoughts are serving us well.

Thinking Scenario
Roisin

Roisin had an insight about the state of mind elevator which she shared with her team. She pointed out that our feelings change because of our thinking and that is normal. We can't expect to always be at high levels of consciousness all day, every day. In the same way you can't expect an elevator to stay on one floor all day. In fact, if you did, you would say it was broken.

Our mind is designed to visit various states of mind, feelings, and thoughts, just as elevators move floors. This is very reassuring to know.

Our thinking process

If we can learn to understand how our thinking system works and agree that every person shares the same thinking operating system, it is possible to see how our separate realities are created. Every person's thinking operating system works in the same way regardless of our cultural identity. Although, normally what we think is culturally and socially conditioned. This is why our thinking influences different world views within each of us.

Basically, it is this simple: we have a thought, we believe that thought - then the thought creates a feeling, and we act from the feeling we are experiencing.

We find this incredibly liberating to know and hope you do also, because it allows us to take back control from our minds and make decisions based on real facts rather than fiction. All it takes is our ability to be aware and conscious in the moment. No big transformation required, just our awareness of how our thinking system works. Knowing about our thinking system provides us with powerful insights at that moment.

Thinking Scenario
Isabelle

Isabelle had recently applied for a promotion and another colleague had been given the job. She recognised that she really allowed her thinking to take her straight to the basement. Her balloon head filled with thoughts like:

- It isn't fair.
- I don't deserve this.
- I'll have to leave now...
- I can't face everyone in the team meeting on Monday.

Then she saw that this was just one possible "thought train" to get on. There were other trains of thought she could consider that might serve her better. This wasn't about being Polly Anna..ish or using positive thinking. It is a simple truth that we don't have to believe all our thinking all the time.

Isabelle remembered that brilliant Victor Frankl quote from Man's Search for Meaning, "Between the stimulus and the response there is always a choice." It is worth remembering that we are always only one insight away from a new experience. We are so much more resilient when we know that a fresh insight can change our experience in any moment.

This space, this gap between reaction and responsiveness can help make positive changes in our lives which will have lasting effects on others around us as well as ourselves. Although, we recommend that you be gentle with yourself as you go back and forth between reactive and responsive, the power is the awareness of where you are at. No one is perfect and being reactive is an unconscious process. Everyone needs constant reminding of how easy it is to slip back into being reactive. After all, we all have been doing this for most of our lives.

As humans, we are constantly being bombarded by our thoughts.

Our minds are always trying to keep us safe, validate ourselves to make us feel good, and to support us in whatever challenge we may face. But sometimes our minds can be too much for us. Sometimes they can get in the way of our goals, or even become a threat to our safety and well-being. This can happen when we think repeatedly about the same thing over and over, causing us to stay awake at night and increase our anxiety. Another example of the treadmill, being stuck on the same thought. The runner starts to feel this overthinking and the result is exhaustion, anxiety and overwhelm.

To jump out of ongoing wheel or trapped thinking, it can be useful to understand more about how our own reality or world view is created.

Let's explore this together further.

CHAPTER EIGHT

CREATING DIFFERENT VIEWPOINTS and our SEPARATE REALITIES

Different viewpoints

The purpose of this section is to help you understand how your worldview affects the way you interact and connect with others. If you want to co-create a team atmosphere where everyone feels like they belong and are valued for who they are as individuals, then we recommend that you work on being open to seeing things from other people's perspectives. Understanding there are various ways to see the world can change the way you experience life.

It is important to remember that being able to see another person's perspective doesn't mean you have to agree with it. This willingness and openness to acknowledge your own views begins with Cultural inQuiry™.

We take the view that whatever we have all been doing up until this point of our lives has been working for us overall because we are here now. The moment we are born, the learning begins as we collect information from our environment, school, society, media, parents, caregivers, family, and so on. Our caregivers and circle of influence share with us all the essential practices and knowledge they have learned throughout their lives that has worked for them. Essentially, we are absorbing **their** beliefs, judgements, stereotypes, and biases innocently without hesitation. We unknowingly just accept their world views as our own personal truth starting from our infant age. The saying, 'it takes a village to raise a child' is true, every person influences us and provides a contribution to our upbringing, our thinking, beliefs, and learnings.

Dr. Cari noted: 'I was so surprised when I thought about this and discovered there are still so many of these beliefs that have remained unquestioned in my life, that I keep believing without hesitation that I never really reflected on until now. In my experience, I would never question something I was brought up to believe until it no longer worked for me in my life or certain circumstances.'

Dr. Cari continues, 'For example, my father started working for a company when he was 19 years old back in the 1960's and started from the bottom and worked throughout his lifetime at the same company. He finally retired with the traditional token of appreciation, the symbolic gold watch, at the age of 65. This used to be the norm, you worked for a single company for your lifetime. When I turned 21, (decades later) my father was getting quite nervous for me since I had not secured a full-time job and I was more interested in having my own business. He could never comprehend that I would not value or pursue a full-time job with an established company for my lifetime career and security. Well simply put, this concept did not exist anymore. I was explaining to my father that I wanted to gain multiple skills so I was adaptable and could work in any environment for any type of company. At this stage of my life, I needed the flexibility for a work-life balance as a single mother which added to the challenge of deciding on a career.

As you can see, even within my own family we had a different belief and view about employment, careers, and financial security.'

Different cultural views happen between different generations, genders, and different levels of education and so on. As well as status, many different components and traits that people get categorised into or labelled as.

It is easy to understand how disagreements and misunderstandings can occur, especially when we are always trying to prove that 'our way' is the best or right way to experience the world. Sometimes that may be true, but most times we don't know or have never experienced a different way.

Conflicts and misunderstandings happen all the time and as parents we say, 'we only want what is best for you', or 'we know what is right because we learned the hard way', and then get frustrated when the child does not go with our way of thinking. The same thing happens in a leadership role, and we believe our way is the only way because we know it based on our experience, then the employee chooses to challenge your view or take a different approach, which causes another form of conflict or power struggle.

In reality, when we think about all types of relationships that we engage in over our lifetime - either a spouse, family, friends, and colleagues, it is easy to see how our personal views can be a barrier to connecting with others. This directly links into our overall personal wellbeing and organisational health.

> Organisational health is based on our individual capacity to recognise and acknowledge this invisible power of our unconscious bias, or automatic pilot, which is formed by a lifetime of cultural conditioning.
>
> *Dr. Cari*

Separate realities

Although in our life experience we recognise that many people can get uncomfortable looking into how and why they see the world a certain way. This is normally because it is something that they have never done before. That is OK. We suggest you kindly accept the challenge and see what you learn.

The good news is that all that is required is the willingness and curiosity to do so. You don't have to change anything about who you are or the way you choose to live your life. For example, such as the traditions you follow, your religion, how you identify yourself with others, or any other lifestyle choice that you thrive on.

We find this so refreshing in a world that is constantly telling us we need to 'transform' our personal life, our exercise routines, our eating habits, or even the way we work and so on and on.

Thinking Scenario
Anika

Anika used to take it really personally if a client didn't call her back when they said they would. She would worry about it for days. It felt like an insult to her and very disrespectful. It also made her doubt her abilities. After learning with CQify, Anika was thinking about how we do not need to take other people's conditioned behaviour and thinking so personally!

Anika loved the concept that each of us is having our own thought created experience in each moment and none of us really can ever know what someone else is truly thinking. She had the insight that she can't know what clients are thinking in each moment. She can't be responsible for their conditioned thinking. These insights felt like freedom to Anika.

She also had the insight that there was no point in her filling up her "balloon head" with thoughts about a client who doesn't call, because then she had to live with that thinking. If she was honest the feelings that this thinking gave her were not pleasant. She had the second insight that she could just let go of these, "why did they do that?" thoughts. She realised that her mind was inventing an infinite number of answers to her questions. However, these answers were all fictions, as she would never be able to know the truth.

As a result of these insights, Anika could dwell on these things a lot less. Sometimes she caught herself thinking about a client and realised, "I'm already a passenger on this thought train". Luckily, she understood that her uncomfortable feelings of frustration were a reminder that she was trying to second guess what was going on in someone else's head, their separate reality. She now understood she could get off that "thought train" if she chose to.

In other words, Anika saw that such thinking was pointless, and she just didn't need to do it if she didn't want to. She really understood that her clients are having a different thought created separate reality and it really was impossible to know what they actually thought about her. Phew! What a relief ☺

To recap, what we are saying is that our personal reality is a product of our own perceptions, values, and beliefs. It is the way we see the world and the way we interact with it. Our personal reality is limited by the cultural conditioning that filters our experiences. This conditioned thinking also shapes our perceptions, attitudes, stereotypes, and beliefs. We are sure you will agree that this is so helpful to know.

The things that happen to us in life are affected by how we think about them. If we believe that something will be difficult or challenging, then it will seem more difficult than if we believe that it will be easy or not hard at all. A similar principle applies to positive outcomes: if we expect something good to happen, then it will seem like a better outcome than if we didn't expect anything at all.

These expectations can be a self-fulfilling prophecy, validating that if we expect something good to happen, then it's more likely that it will because we'll act differently as though it already has happened (i.e., smiling broadly when someone asks us how our day went).

Similarly, if we expect something bad to happen, then that may also come true because of how it impacts our behaviour and attitudes. Our life experience helps to guide us as we navigate the world around us. It helps us make sense of the world, but it can also be limiting through our own cultural lens.

As adults, we usually find ourselves surrounded by other people who see things differently than we do or who have different experiences than ours. These differences can lead to conflict because they create tension between two perspectives which may be very different from each other. The more two perspectives differ, the greater risk of a disagreement between the people.

Then normally an argument can occur, causing various reactions until one side wins out over another or the other simply walks away. Lots of times people will just drop out of our lives and we do not really notice why. That person who just quits their job one day, or that friend who no longer calls you back. What we notice is that people in general do not like conflict and will try to avoid any form of confrontation. The tactics to win revert to protecting our own egos, so a simple negotiation can turn into a physical fight, bullying or any other forms of intimidation.

Another way that our lives shape our perceptions is through culture: culture informs the way we dress, speak, work, socialise, interact, raise our families, build relationships, define roles, determine behaviours, our language, customs, rituals and many more aspects. This is what is called our cultural conditioning.

Thinking Scenario
Tareq

Tareq had difficulty with a colleague who was working on a project with him. The colleague's emails were very short and succinct and Tareq experienced them as rude, cold, and hostile. He had the insight that this may be a case of "seperate realities" and that perhaps the email style the colleague used was just different to his own. They worked in different parts of the world after all and had different cultural references.

Tareq noticed a feeling of genuine amusement when he saw how much time he was wasting judging and disliking this colleague who he had never met. Was he really this upset just because they had a separate reality about the etiquette of how to write emails?

Tareq realised that it would make things simpler when he got these emails if he chose to just smile to himself and think, "*Well I wouldn't write one like that.*" He didn't have to be hurt by it or offended. He could just write back in his own style and leave it at that.... It would be nice not to have a sinking feeling every time he saw his colleague's name in his inbox.

Social influences also shape our perceptions, behaviours, beliefs, the way we dress, speak, build relationships, our attitudes towards things, money, education and so on. Our social conditioning happens through media, at our school, work, or community, friends, and the communities where we live.

Our social and cultural conditioning is constantly shaping our biases, stereotypes, beliefs, and judgements.

Ladder of inference

The ladder of inference is a model that explains how we process biased information to make decisions throughout our day. When we have a situation, we normally react to, automatically our balloon inflates instantly without really thinking about it..... we tend to go on our 'gut instinct' or make instant decisions based on our past.

We tend to focus on what we know, and then use it as a basis for drawing conclusions about what we don't know. As you may have experienced, this can be very risky and increase our chances of making the wrong choice or coming to the wrong conclusion. We do this subconsciously because it helps us make sense of the world. We want to keep life simple, and it is a lot easier to focus on what seems obvious than to try and figure out how everything works together.

But there's a problem with this approach: it can lead us astray when we're trying to make important decisions. It can limit our curiosity to seek out new perspectives or information. This is why it is so important to understand how we process and filter information around us.

Here is a good graphic explanation of the process we are discussing below:

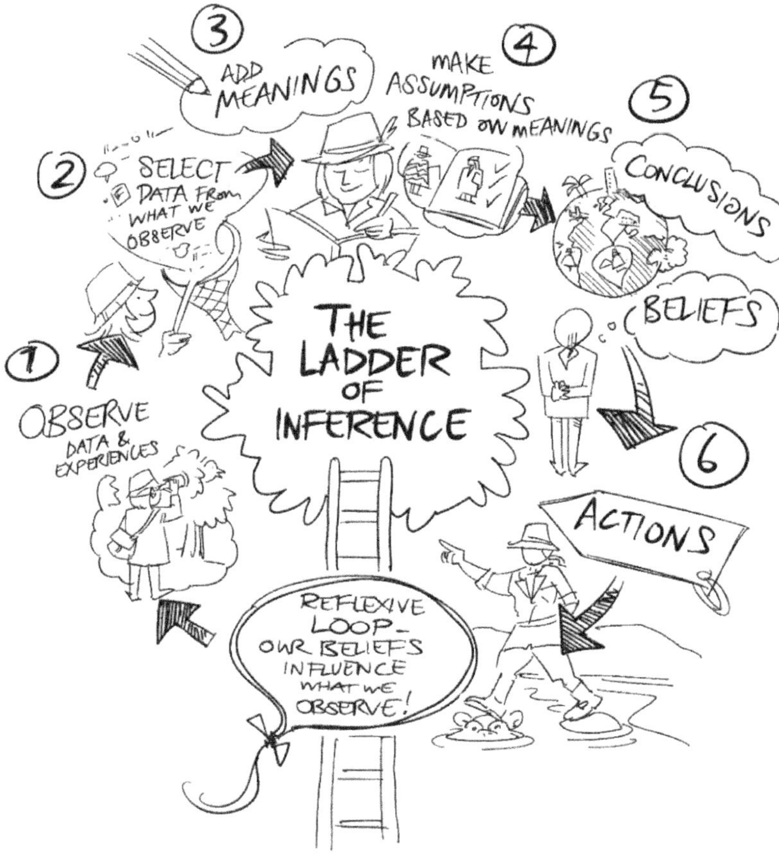

Now this ladder of inference is nothing new, but we wanted to share with you so you can see how easily we automatically base our decision making on assumptions based on past experiences or our perception of existing information. Again, these associations happen instantaneously. We like this model. It simply shows that once we are aware of the beliefs that we use to interpret the world, we can also disrupt the cycle and be open to new information.

Can you think of any situations where you realised that you just got it wrong? You reacted hurt or angry to something someone said or did? Then realised it had nothing to do with you, once they explained you were able to replace criticism with empathy and humility?

What would happen if we could catch ourselves to explore these options before we had a full reaction, before our balloon filled up? What would happen if we learned to take a pause and check ourselves to see how the situation is triggering us? Remember how we discussed pausing and shifting to responsiveness?

Now imagine if we apply this to our daily decision making during our interactions with colleagues. How does this inspire humility and vulnerability?

Let's consider what would happen if we applied it to being a leader that navigates a chaotic or complex business landscape ......would this be called an Egoless Leader? Possibly, except now we know how easily we can encourage labelling and judgement because that is how our mind is associating new experiences with old ones.

We would recommend seeking connection with others with humility and curiosity as opposed to assumptions.

If you could already apply what we have shared so far like, being responsive, bringing your awareness to the moment to curiously experience yourself and others, how does this impact your world view now? Is it limiting, or does it expand potential possibilities? Or does it inspire to be more OPEN and curious about others? Or do you fear difference and try to look for the comfort of people that have similar attributes? It is a nice place to reflect and acknowledge your thinking.

CQ Exercise:

Take a moment to ask yourself the question:

What have I learned about being responsive?

About being self-aware and curious around experiences?

When we reflect, it is always amazing to see what each of us 'see'. Consider adding to your thoughts to your journal. Coming back to our journals periodically to review our notes shows where we have grown in ourselves, how we changed our thinking and self-awareness.

CQ Exercise:

Take a moment and reflect on your answers.

Are you open to change and other's perceptions?

Has your curiosity been triggered?

Or is fear blocking your life experiences?

Reflecting on this insight.... did you know that you automatically accept another's perception or world view unconditionally as a child? We innocently believe everything our caregivers, families, teachers, and circle of influence tell us at our young age. This knowledge naturally will work for you until it does not. It may even take something more unexpected such a divorce, illness or losing someone special to jolt us into opening up to see another perspective.

To shift our unconscious biases requires our willingness to accept new knowledge around the topic and openly investigate truth as opposed to opinion. Life lessons for one individual doesn't mean that is the best for you... so why don't we challenge what we think we already know? Or what we learn?

An example Dr. Cari shares is what her father 'accepted as his version of how reality worked was valid specifically for him, based on his own circumstances, skills, parents, culture, education, attitude, and perceptions. His intention was to pass on the most valuable life lessons he experienced so that she would not repeat the same mistakes he did. He wanted her to be safe, protected, happy and successful because he loved her so much as a daughter'.

She also learned what is important to consider respectfully is that even a father and daughter are separate individual people. She was raised in a different time, with different technology available to her, with access to new information, with her own personal talents, likes and perceptions. She is her own unique person. Especially now as an adult, it is clear to her that she has her own beliefs, perceptions and separate reality or world view.

Equally, this applies to both professional and personal development, we should be teaching ourselves, our teams, our children how to be relentlessly curious by asking questions, researching, seeking answers, and embracing being themselves. We can then understand that different versions of reality exist, not only the version we are personally experiencing. Everyone has their own version of reality, which is OK because we can still share similar core values. This is called **separate realities** just as we explained earlier.

When we meet up to play a new board game with our friends or family members, the first thing we do is ask who played this game before.... if some have and some have not..... we read out the rules so everyone knows how to play the game, and everyone can follow the same rules. Why would a fight or disagreement happen?

This is when someone interprets a rule differently than the other players, right? So how can we overcome or prevent that from happening? This is the key question. This is where leaders innocently struggle without potentially realising the core issue that is ongoing or repeatedly happening.

The struggle can end when we can acknowledge this is because people have different ways of understanding, processing, or undertaking information or expected actions based on their unique perceptions.

To imagine that all people see things the same way you do is a big mistake. It is necessary to be curious, that there are other ways of doing things than the way you do that is perfectly acceptable. It is also important to allow ourselves to be vulnerable so that we can be open to learning about others by letting them learn about us as individuals. The social mask, pretending to agree, pretending to like or do something to belong is not being authentic and, surprisingly, can end up being more exclusive as a result. When we can be vulnerable, we can be responsive in the situation so we can also reflect in the moment.

For example, everything we have learned along the way has brought us each to this point, so something we are doing must be working. We are always learning in some way, unconsciously or consciously.

As opposed to fearing people that do things differently or look different, we are always curious to learn how and why instead of criticising.

What if we all replaced Criticism with Empathy...

How would this improve our connection with others?

What do you think?

Assessing our current state of mind

The key is to be able to assess your current state of mind while understanding how it is influencing your current world view. If your state of mind is in the basement (remember the elevator thinking 'earlier in the book') when we are having our team meeting, you won't be able to contribute your most creative self. Instead, you will be more negative, thinking about other things, asking yourself if you even like your job and spiral downward. Not the best state of mind to contribute to the meeting.

Alternatively, if you come bouncing in on being on the upper floor levels of state of mind, everything takes on a new energy and perspective. Recognising that our state of mind can fluctuate moment to moment, is very empowering and helps us be more compassionate towards ourselves and others. This personal awareness is so helpful to understand our own thinking and moods. We also want to point out that it is OK to be in whatever state of mind you are in. We all experience all levels most of the time and being aware of where you are in the elevator can help improve how you communicate with others.

Thinking Scenario
Ling

Ling really noticed the power of separate realities at play when she had been part of an interview panel team.

One of the candidates had arrived 30 minutes late and explained that their train had been delayed. The candidate then gave a great interview performance. Ling's boss (who was also on the panel) was adamant that the candidate's lateness was unacceptable and insisted that they shouldn't be offered the job on that basis.

Ling would have usually been furious with her boss, but she realised that he was having reactive thinking.

So, she simply asked him, "If you didn't know this candidate had arrived late would you offer him the job?"

Her boss acknowledged that he would.

She then asked, "So, could you have some insight about that?"

She smiled as she said it, her boss just laughed and said, "*separate realities, eh?...Nice one...*"

At this point the boss and the whole panel decided to offer the candidate the job.

The candidate turned out to be a brilliant colleague who was never late.

Recognising that we are all experiencing separate realities based on fluctuating states of mind, we realise just how similar we all are. We can then connect and empathise with one another on a deeper level. We no longer believe our instant judgements or automatic criticisms because we are now curious to know about the person, not what the conditioned cultural stereotypes say.

Dr. Cari's research[5] emphasises that our individual world views, beliefs, and stereotypes can be challenged and changed when willing to explore new information and experiences.

Dr. Jacqui agrees, we evolve in our thinking over time based on our experiences and information we absorb. By reflecting on why we think the way we think helps us to take that information and turn it into knowledge, our worldview, somewhat like how a good wine matures over time.

Pause + Reflection = Robust decisions

Now a key question is how does this all relate to organisational leadership and management?

Organisational leadership and management

The missing link between achieving optimal organisational psychological health and achieving holistic performance results is based on how willing each individual is to ***unlearn*** and **embrace** the potential barriers and possibilities of our personal reality. When we can respect that we all have separate realities, and no one is better than any other.

Our realities are formed from a mixture of influences, perceptions and experiences that are unique to each of us. This is so pivotal to understand

and takes the pain out of communication with other people. We can now surrender to trying to manipulate or convince ourselves or others to believe our way of thinking.

We understand we can never know what our next thought will be, but we are no longer powerless to our thoughts.

Once this is achieved as a team, the **agility ability**™ of everyone flourishes and thrives on change.

The team can be free to flow like a river over rocks with no obstacles getting in the way of implementing plans.

CHAPTER NINE

MOVING BEYOND CULTURAL TRANSFORMATION to attain AGILITY ABILITY™

From cultural transformation to next level performance

The majority of leaders agree that a great strategy is very important to business performance. The blind spot is knowing that without an agile organisational culture at the core, these plans will most likely fail to be implemented. Stakeholders need to be engaged by being personally aligned with the organisation's purpose and vision because they have a voice in co-creating it. What we know is that if the team is not feeling connected, they will not execute the plan.

On our evidenced based insights from decades of practical experience, we have come to realise that there is so much ambiguity or general confusion in what can contribute to business success.

Especially now in a glocalised world, where people have so many different cultural identities and are attempting to collaborate as a team. The legacy organisations, or the ones that have been around for decades are more vulnerable to keeping policies and procedures in place over a longer period of time. We encourage regular review of guidelines, laws, regulations, etc to make sure they are relevant and fit for purpose.

The challenge is that, through our individual lens, these 'rules' or language used could mean something different to every one of us. It could be that the original board of directors created these policies and procedures decades ago, within a completely different work environment. Normal business practice was most likely different then compared to now.

How often are the policies and procedures reviewed and revised at your organisation? Then the next question is, by who? Are there multiple perspectives considered across the organisation or only at board level?

This is why there is so much confusion, as there is this invisible assumption that we all think various terms mean the same thing and that the 'rules' are clear to everyone. Which is definitely not the case, as discovered in Dr. Cari's research[5].

Looking at the rules, terms, or policies from this perspective, we can clearly see how easy misunderstandings can happen. The different interpretations could cause confusion which can result with conflict between team members. Part of the Cultural inQuiry process is taking time to gain a consensus of meanings and definitions used.

An organisation can be great and achieve lofty heights, but without a strong agile organisational culture, it will never reach its full potential, it will falter and potentially fail. Executive actions speak louder than words in creating an organisation's culture.[6,12]

Dr. Jacqui

Ambiguity

Ambiguity refers to the general misunderstandings that commonly occur in all forms of communication. A great example is when we look closely at job descriptions, value statements, company policies and similar tools, one can see why leaders are drowning in ambiguity (confusion) mainly because of the different perceptions attached to various titles and labels.

It is common to see job descriptions call for:

- **strong** leaders,
- **good** communicators,
- team players,
- motivated,
- great with people,
- Positive attitude,
- Hard worker,
- Reliable,
- Responsible.

But when we all start to say what we think these terms mean, it will be discovered quickly that meanings are all influenced by our individual perceptions. We may think a team player or good communicator means something different to our colleagues.

It is interesting to see how biases can influence our behaviours. For example, when we are hiring, and the applicant went to the same school or shares similar interests, it's our human instinct to feel more attracted to people that we perceive to be similar to ourselves. This perception or worldview is impacted by *affinity bias*, where we are attracted to people, we perceive are like us. There are hundreds of different kinds of biases all that contribute to our cultural conditioning and world view.

We all have bias and that is not a bad thing, it's inevitable.

This is the shortcut our minds use that helps us make sense of the world around us. The main problems arise when we don't acknowledge that biases exist and are influencing us unconsciously all the time. This is ingrained into our automatic pilot. Then we stay stuck and keep assuming people are sharing the same meaning that we intended or that they understand exactly what we mean.

When we ask another person, 'do you understand what I mean' and they reply 'yes', we would always ask for the other person to share what they heard each of us say.

It's always surprising to us to hear their interpretation of what we said. Even as expert communicators, we have misunderstandings. This is because our skills are helpful, but they can never intercept how another person's perception filters and processes information.

Ambiguity is the common
denominator in misunderstandings.

Dr. Cari

The true source of interpersonal conflict

What we realised is that so many misunderstandings are occurring, and we are not even aware of them. Conflict within teams or between individuals affects all aspects of developing human-to-human connections in the workplace. Our balloon heads are inflating without us even understanding why we are triggered.

Recognising how conflict can sabotage organisations that have implemented several policies, procedures, and tools to assist people with overcoming internal conflicts with other team members. Sadly, regardless of these measures, conflict is still one of the main reasons people leave or become 'quiet quitters'[16] through increased sick leave and poor performance.

Conflict is simply a misunderstanding on steroids.

It is a misunderstanding that has grown into something larger normally fuelled by anger, bitterness, apathy, resentment, jealousy, anxiety, or even depression. Conflict is a major root cause of poor performance that starts at an individual level and then affects the whole organisation.

Did you know that being a balloon head can be contagious?

CiQ We were then keen to investigate: Why is there nothing helping to reduce this ongoing silent pandemic within most organisations?

When we begin to explore where conflict comes from it is easy to see how a simple misunderstanding can propel out of control based on individual reactions to a situation. Just like we shared during the balloon head video.

An interesting observation we made is that conflict management solutions appear to be missing a critical component, **Cultural inQuiry**™. It is not useful to expend time and energy, active listening and applying empathy in an effort to understand another's perspective without a foundational understanding about our own personal worldview. Understanding how our cultural and social conditioning is essential to being more culturally sensitive. Then we can begin to actively listen and be more empathetic when we know about our separate realities. This makes a huge impact on communication so we can be open to understanding each other or at least flag up when there is a misunderstanding happening.

Only then can we begin to dismantle our personal bias or open ourselves to alternative facts or information. It must be noted that our social and cultural programming begins at birth, and it feels natural, comfortable, and effortless to function from this perspective. The journey to unlearning some of the programming that is a hindrance to progressive engagement begins with reflecting on the beliefs we have. Then it is about having the courage, commitment, and resilience to let the ones go that are no longer required or get replaced with new ones. It is an active way to be less reactive and more responsive.

Active listening is an essential part of a conversation. As we have experienced, active listening is a great intention to start with but surprisingly does not reduce misunderstandings. It is only part of the solution. This is because even if we are actively listening, our own perceptions and balloon heads are disrupting the interpretation of the message.

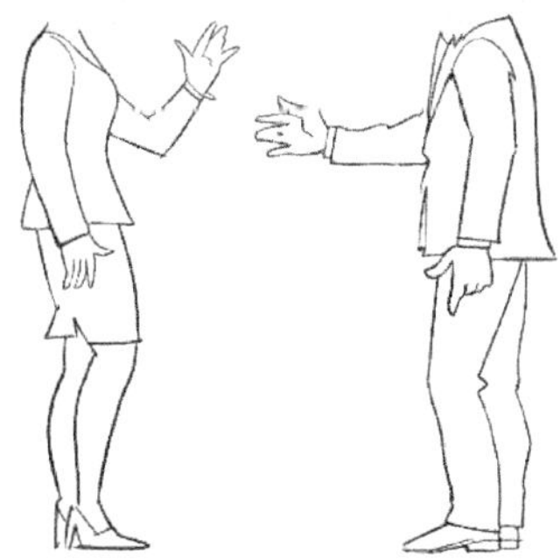

Let's look at a series of short exercises to build your knowledge base on how your thoughts and beliefs guide your judgement.

CQ Exercise:

To evaluate your own beliefs, values and perceptions let's use a writing exercise. Take a piece of paper and draw a line down the middle, top to bottom. On the left, write 'what I said' and on the right 'what they said'.

What I said	What they said

Think of a challenging conversation you have had, one where you don't believe your view was wrong but there was a disconnect between you and the other person.

Then write down your perception of what happened in that conversation, separating what you said on the left-hand side and what they said on the right-hand side. On the left also document what you were thinking at that moment and why you believe you were right.

Potentially, you may see the difference between blame and accountability emerge, or maybe something different.

CQ Exercise:

Have you ever considered why some people like to blame others for their own situation? Blame is an ingredient of automatic pilot, designed to protect egos, but not useful. The thought that our way is better than the other is regressive.

Leaders must be clear on their own emotional triggers that are not relevant at the time. A helpful tool we refer to as: ***My Inner Voice Says...*** this puts conversations we have had into perspective when we are reflecting on them. This is a tool that speaks of the inner thinking often not shared in public but which the opinion holder holds dear.

This exercise can assist with critical self-reflection as it acknowledges judgement, interpretations, and hidden thinking. Done well, it can help overcome conflict.

> Between stimulus and response there is a space. **In that space is our power to choose our response.** In our response lies our growth and our freedom.
>
> *Viktor Frankl*[57]

For this exercise take the output of Exercise 1 and place a line across the page under the last entry. Add two new headings. 'My inner voice says' on the left and 'So what does this mean' on the right.

My inner voice says	So what does this mean

Add what your inner voice is saying, your thoughts, beliefs, and feelings about the event in the left-hand column. There is no right or wrong here, so be as blunt and detailed as you can.

Take a short few minutes' break. Dr. Jacqui takes time out to make a cup of coffee to ponder on what her inner voice has been saying. Dr. Cari prefers a cup of tea or glass of water.

When you are ready, think about what you have written in the left-hand column. Read and reread it. Think about how this makes you feel, why you are thinking the way you are. Is there a history with this person, previous conflict, business dealings, staff engagement or friendship that has been affected by the conversation?

Then write your answer in the right-hand column. Consider how this reflects to others, how this affects the relationship and outcome. Is there anything you need to reconsider or change in your thinking, response, behaviour?

Questions could also include:

- Am I taking anything for granted?
- Am I holding onto something I need to let go of?
- What do I need to change about my thinking?
- Why is this important to me?

This exercise is about the 'me', what I think, why I think that way and what I need to do about it. Once I understand 'me', I can then understand 'we'.

This can then be punctuated with good listening skills. People believe in their perceptions, overt or covert, normally without acknowledging the conflict is based on different interpretations of the situation but without fundamental justification. It is used to divert the individual from the core issue of feeling any form of discomfort or inadequacy.

> We **think** we listen, but very **rarely** do we **listen with real understanding**, true empathy. Yet, [active] listening of this very special kind, is one of the most potent forces for change that I know.
>
> *Carl Rogers*[55]

Accordingly, active listening is a focus on what is being "said" to discover the difference in what is "heard" once it is decoded according to everyone's perspective of it. Immediate automatic judgement is natural. It is then followed by the belief that the support assumptions are a true reality without scrutinising, more often believing in the worst-case scenario.

To shake up this thought pattern it is necessary to be self-aware and listen actively. What is important is to separate our own emotional triggers from the past to consciously experience the current moment more clearly. We cannot rely on active listening alone to improve communication. It is essential that we first explore our own cultural lens that creates our worldview.

What if we replaced **judgement** with **curiosity and humility**?

Dr. Cari

People have several different cultural imprints within them that are difficult to separate from without acknowledgement. It, therefore, becomes important to replace judgement with curiosity, giving the other party the benefit of the doubt. For mutual understanding, we each must endeavour to trust, feel safe to express ourselves, ask questions and speak openly to ensure mutual understanding.

When conversations are actively reviewed through different lenses it can cause a reaction if something is unfamiliar. When the consequences of trying to solve new problems with traditional ways of thinking is not going to work. Einstein said it best:

We cannot solve our problems
with the same thinking
we used when we created them.

Albert Einstein

If this is the case then what is the formula to overcoming this confusion or ambiguity within organisational communication, leadership, strategy, and overall performance?

From leadership to a co-creator ethos

It is now time to evolve from a focus on leadership development towards a co-creator ethos that embraces every individual to inform the new rules and language used within the organisation. This is what we call a ***systemic reflection,*** where the existing policies and procedures have an overhaul with fresh eyes and thinking. This collective input from the team makes sure there is clarity by creating unified definitions of commonly used values and terms to replace assumptions. The insights generated during this activity have a powerful place to generate new rules more suitable for today's ecosystem and complex environment.

The co-creator role or description is all encompassing to everyone in the organisation. Our hybrid working models are seeking greater accountability and autonomy, rather than conventional leadership. When we show up with an intention to work within a team, research validates that it is with different perceived attitudes and behaviours than being the leader.

We do understand that this is a new way of thinking and goes against all that is out there now driving leadership development in business schools and organisations. Keeping in mind that everything being taught and encouraged will be helpful to go to the next level as a co-creator, so nothing is ever wasted. Learning is always ongoing with new concepts that are developed based on improving existing ones. We are simply encouraging an opportunity to reimagine how collaboration can occur to unite people towards achieving the best version of themselves to accomplish the team's visions.

We invite you to get curious and read further.

For clarity, we are defining leadership in this context as the capability of leading a group of individuals to impact all stakeholders by motivating and inspiring effective action towards achieving desired organisational objectives[13].

We are suggesting that leadership requires upskilling to become co-creators to successfully navigate within a hybrid glocalised team.

Every day we hear of a new offering to develop leadership skills, which we are sure you have heard of at least some of the following leadership styles: authentic, servant, situational, autocratic, democratic, laissez-faire, transformational, charismatic, collaborative, visionary, strategic, action-centred, active, empathetic, compassionate, coaching, egoless, conscious, reflective, and so on.

These styles are used interchangeably but they all have their key attributes and competencies. The definition of leadership and the application of leadership skills is skewed by different interpretations that depend on the individual's perception of life experiences, cultural identities, and beliefs. Leadership styles have been adapted throughout the past decades to meet the evolving needs of organisations. The big gap is that now uncertainty and complexities are the norm, making a zig zag or nonlinear impact in risk assessments, as opposed to historically when it was a predictable steady climb or decline.

To be successful, it is no longer the sole responsibility of how we traditionally view that ***one great leader.*** It is already the collective responsibility of everyone.

The continual leadership challenge is navigating daily situations when people all have different problems. The leader is expected to determine what style of leadership is best suited in every unique situation, in addition to managing their own responsibilities and job function.

This is an IMPOSSIBLE expectation on any leader.

You would have to be a superhero mind reader to master this skill to meaningfully lead others in the moment exactly the way they need you to be.

Imagine what happens if you are the leader and you have 10, 20, 50 people or more on your team. We now know we all have separate realities and fluctuating states of minds....... how big does your balloon go with this stress and anxiety as you struggle to meet your own KPI's, be innovative and push towards team performance?

This could be the reason that new leadership styles keep popping up in the attempt to fill this gap with a magic formula.

Although, not one specific style can capture the importance of our individual cultural identities as the sweet spot in people management and organisational performance.

Current research confirms that there is no best leadership style[14,15] for this new era because now we are rethinking leadership as we know it. The true mastery for today is about the understanding about the way we connect with others and CO-CREATE **as a team.**

Let's take a look how people currently describe a great leader:

What do you notice, what words stand out?

We like to point out the words like power, influence, intelligence, responsibility, followers, success, and decision-making.

Let's look how this compares to being a great team player or as we say, a co-creator.

LEADER	CO-CREATOR
Power	Knowledge sharing
Authority	Collaboration
Influence	Consensus
Intelligence	Connection
Responsibility	Accountability
Followers	Synergy
Isolated decision-making	Collective decision making
Profitability	Performance
Individual	Team
Dominance	Authenticity
Systems focused	People focused

> Society, schools, and businesses are still looking at leadership as something we DO to others, when in reality, it is more useful to be a co-creator who can form a connection with a diverse range of people and work in collaboration to achieve a team in FLOW – this is what is required now and for the future.
>
> *Dr. Cari*

In this current new world of working, we need highly adaptive individuals who can shift roles easily and connect with others as a team to meet the new demands in today's glocal economy. Collaboration and harmony are vital.

Today's edge-walker is a phrase we identified that describes how global leaders are embracing and shifting towards this new non-leadership paradigm of CO-CREATORS to successfully manage the complexities of *glocal* teams.

What exactly is a co-creator anyway?

Co-creator

A co-creator instigates a new flavour and energy into a team and organisation as a whole. It is a different way to individually contribute with impact and value to your team. A co-creator is connected authentically to themselves first, then towards the cause and purpose of the organisation. Co-creation is recognising equal personal growth opportunities that are rewarded as being part of a team in their flow.

Showing up as a co-creator opens us up to engage, generate and align diverse perspectives. When individuals embrace the role as a co-creator it is possible to collectively drive meaning and impactful outcomes.

Everyone works together to foster a culture that is agile, adaptive, and responsive to ongoing uncertainty while remaining in flow.

What is a team that flows?

Team flow

We are not talking about sunshine, rainbows, and unicorns here. A co-creator can still experience misunderstandings, conflict, and barriers we discussed earlier. Teams can still be vulnerable to tantrums, ego flare ups and hidden agendas.

The difference is how Cultural inQuiry™ can enhance your overall human experience in your personal life and at work.

The difference is that individuals and teams no longer get stuck on the hamster wheel or treadmill and can surf ongoing changes like the perfect wave.

The difference is everyone is aware of how to recognise their current state of mind and how to release their balloon filled with stress, anxiety and overwhelm. People know how they can return to a state of calm.

Everyone knows they can overcome any barrier by being responsive and discovering fresh insights in every situation.

When we are all co-creators. It eliminates the invisible power struggles, a game our egos love to play. The understanding of the impact on personal and organisational performance overrides any intentions to revert to hidden agendas or self-sabotaging patterns.

Achieving the ultimate organisational flow means that most of the members are seamlessly in a state of synchronised creativity and collaboration. The foundation of achieving this level of psychological safety requires responsive team communication.

Moving from Me to We

We are already experiencing just how co-creative teams can fast track implementation of plans simply due to stakeholder involvement, alignment, and accountability. Leadership is already being replaced with co-creators because organisational success is no longer about a sole individual initiative, but a collective one.

We must emphasise that being a co-creator involves our personal **agility ability**™ to reflect in action, to be consciously in the moment, to reveal the connection with others. It goes deeper than acknowledging our emotions towards how to empower through our open expression of our thinking.

Once we can all make the shift toward a co-creating workplace culture, having buy-in can influence its own environment or eco-system that perpetuates ongoing collaboration at a new level of impact.

This organisational flow can create unlimited performance outcomes because creativity is at the heart of action.

This involves working with your team, which needs to be part of the foundations of the organisational culture, turning these new actions into a progressive 'that's just how we do things around here'.

> Where teams become part of developing the foundations of organisational culture through co-creation to become a natural process, it embeds the cultural change into the very fabric of an organisation, achieving sustainable change.[6,10,11,12,23]
>
> *Dr. Jacqui*

CQ It is recommended that the silos or divisions within the organisations come together to collectively work towards the same vision. Easier said than done. Dr. Jacqui has run cross-organisational sessions in vision and mission setting as part of developing business strategies and finds it surprising the range of silo thinking that remains within organisations.

In our view, it is why so many organisations are unable to implement their plans. Even with a focus to guide the investment into quality people that contribute positively to the trust-based culture of your company, the reality is that there will always be levels of misunderstandings.

Co-creation framework

The insight led communication framework used that supports co-creating teams is called LENS:

Our **LENS Framework**™ co-creates the foundation of building connections and clarity with others. Thereafter, you'll find that everything else falls into place. It is a form of reset, a cultural transformation that goes beyond everything many know right now.

To explain further:

Leveraging culture to - explore and acknowledge our own individual schema. This understanding needs to include how everyone has different cultural conditioning that is influencing their own view of the world.

This is the first stage of the framework that is completed by using Cultural inQuiry™ to begin this individual journey about understanding ourselves on a deeper level. This is a learning journey that is continuous. When we are in a flow of personal development it is because we have relentless curiosity about ourselves and others. With humility we can contribute to a co-created intention and purpose that will help improve our world.

Leveraging culture is connecting people who:

- Embrace curiosity about themselves and others,
- Care with intention and purpose, and
- Thrive on continuous learning.

Encourage - this is a place that is created within the team and organisation that is considered to be psychologically safe to show up as our authentic selves. Encouraging ourselves and others to focus on personal and professional growth and development. Understanding that one does not happen without the other.

This is the second stage of the framework where Cultural inQuiry is integrated into understanding how to co-create these spaces and learning opportunities. This is working under the premise that not everyone will perceive the safe space in the same way. In addition, to encourage personal and professional growth will require a deeper inquiry into the understanding what the bespoke needs are within all key stakeholder groups.

Encourage is making space to:

- Nurture a psychologically safe place to connect,
- Focus on personal and professional growth and development.

Non-judgemental Insights – this is where the magic happens with the unexpected inspiration and ideas from the team. Insights are personal ideas that have no specific formula. Insights are formulated in freedom where your mind has unlimited access to all possibilities and not confined by expectation.

This is the third stage of the framework where Cultural inQuiry is designed specifically to focus on how to generate non-judgmental insights. This is not a simple as it may seem, this is where people can get stuck. There are many different points that must join together to get this stage to thrive. We can relate this to the surfer waiting in the ocean for that perfect wave to ride.

Non-judgemental insights is the perfect wave to:

- Be responsive and generate creative ideas through a collective team effort towards a vision,
- Fostering collaboration within an inclusive team environment.

Strategy Implementation - putting those plans into action and overcoming the day-to-day distractions.

This final stage of the framework is based on our **insight-led action inquiry cycles©** which unleashes co-creating high performing teams. This is also explained in Part 3 as part of the roadmap section. This is when collaboration peaks at the top of the mountain with a full view for co-created culture-based performance.

The view from the peak:

- Regardless of any barriers there is a relentless team flow that is resilient, adaptable and sustainable.

CHAPTER TEN
RESETTING THE ORGANISTIONAL CULTURE

Organisational culture agility

Agile organisations can seize opportunities quickly by adapting to changing stakeholder needs. With advanced feedback cycles that gauge marketplace challenges and opportunities, agility enables holistic collaboration across all departments. Due to the fast-paced dynamic business landscape, a culture united by purpose is destined to truly thrive.

Organisational agility is not a one size fits all concept. Agility essentially starts from our personal inner agility first, just like we are sharing in this book. This bespoke nature of structuring a culture, positioned for rapid innovation with sustainability, then requires teams that can flow.

Teams are made up of individuals.

Now you can begin to reimagine how to build organisational agility.

High performing teams are anchored by insight-led communication over prescriptive techniques. Remembering that prescriptive techniques are about lists, steps, or specific directions, just like we would use in a lifesaving emergency. The difference is within an organisational setting these techniques only smother creativity. Using insight-led communication is what creates those surprising ideas that can overcome any perceived obstacle. Individual development embeds the possibilities of unlimited learning opportunities within a team. Learning is the current that turns into the wave of a sustainable co-created team flow.

As co-creators we know that everyone on the team will always be:

- At different stages of personal growth,
- Riding the state of mind elevator,
- Vulnerable to ego flare ups,
- Experiencing a separate reality to others.

Now we can begin to understand the direct link from our inner agility to organisational agility. With everyone at a different stage of personal growth, there is no need to try for a collective organisational transformation that is inspired from the top or the leadership team. The only small change that it is required is to create a safe space for individual insights to occur. Then these individual shifts can open up towards a willingness to learn that we all have separate realities and that is OK. Then we can stop putting energy into trying to convince everyone there is only one way.

> It is with the collection of different perspectives co-creators can influence a powerful innovative culture reset to achieve organisational agility.
>
> *Dr. Cari*

But first, let's unpack what it means to create a sustainable cultural reset, that so many leadership executives (co-creators) desire.

What is an organisational culture reset?

Resetting the culture

At its most basic level, a cultural reset is a shift in the way that people think and behave within the organisation. This is where most leadership teams get stuck, in our experience.

Getting stuck can be caused by a number of different factors, including changes in leadership, new technology, economic shifts, people leaving or the arrival of new employees. In an organisational context, cultural transformation refers to a change in culture that occurs within an organisation as a result of its practices, policies and measurement tools. Additionally, the key driver of these policies and practices would be centred around Key Performance Indicators (KPI's)[2], Objectives Key Results (OKR's)[3,] a Balanced Scorecard[4] and profitability. This would be considered a **performance-based culture.** This can be challenging to shift because it involves changing habits and beliefs that have been ingrained in employees for years by their managers, colleagues, and other influential stakeholders.

Shifting an organisation's culture is often associated with organisational change management (OCM), which involves creating strategies for managing employee behaviour through changes such as mergers or acquisitions. OCM also refers to managing employee resistance to change, which can lead to conflict between teams and team members[6,10,11].

This can occur when there is disagreement about how best to implement changes within departments or divisions within an organisation's structure. Changes could include issues such as pay cuts or job losses due to restructuring processes taking place. Within larger companies such as banks or manufacturing firms owned by multinational conglomerates, stock prices may be falling due to poor performance at retail outlets across regional markets or worldwide.

Dr. Jacqui has led, been involved in, and developed from inception organisational change in departments, divisions, and whole organisations in both public and private sectors over the last thirty years. From her experience and research, organisational change management is only one small aspect but a potentially significant pain point. Unless staff are engaged and communication channels are open, misunderstanding can surface quickly, creating a minefield to navigate. It is the very underpinning ecosystem that needs to change.

Change that challenge the very fabric of an organisation's culture, creates a wave that shifts the ecosystem.

Dr. Jacqui

When we talk about a cultural shift, it's easy to think that it's all about changing the way people think and behave to improve the overall employee experience. But organisational culture is more than just a shared set of values: it's an entire system of beliefs and long-term practices that are so ingrained in your organisation, that they become an invisible set of rules that act as the main operating system.

When you start thinking about culture this way, it becomes clear that if you want to change your organisation's culture, conventionally, you need to be prepared for a long-term commitment.

It is possible that using prescriptive techniques can produce some small or even larger changes in the short term, but those changes normally will eventually fade away and old habits or patterns will resume. We both agree that unless there is a core connection between the individual and organisational values, these efforts are not robust enough to sustain any type of change in most cases. We are aiming to increase your awareness and understanding about the high-level process and barriers shared above with a **performance-based culture**.

Moving from performance-based culture to culture-based performance

We will begin to introduce the advantages of co-creating **culture-based performance.** Once everyone has increased their awareness about separate realities and improved their inner agility, it is possible to begin to integrate Cultural inQuiry™ further into the team context. Cultural inQuiry promotes engagement, connection, and individual contribution that will motivate everyone to work towards the agreed co-created vision or goal.

This improved level of accountability and performance is based on increasing the overall experience of acceptance, humility and empathy that is the foundation of this desired culture. It is when the culture of the organisation is designed around the needs and input of the stakeholders, culture-based performance can be achieved. In simple terms, the goal is for all team members to actively contribute, feel more engaged, connected, and motivated, which will encourage them to show up and give their best efforts in their daily tasks. In our experience, it is possible to make this shift with measurable and sustainable impact.

> In moving an organisation from performance-based culture to culture-based performance, the underpinning ecosystem needs to change. The human factor in co-creating the future reality is a core component of that ecosystem.
>
> *Dr. Jacqui*

The ultimate goal is to reset your culture by unleashing your personal (inner), team and organisational **agility ability**™ to generate your and your organisation's **culture-based performance**!™

Let's continue this learning journey in Part Two.

CQ KEY INSIGHTS OF PART ONE

In summary, the key insights, or takeaways from Part One include:

- ✓ The world is continuing to become more complex.
- ✓ Today's reality requires new insights and a fresh way of interrogating problems.

- ✓ Identifying the true source of the problem can be a big challenge for leaders.
- ✓ Barriers such as fear, masks, and egos can keep us in a reactive mode.
- ✓ We need to be aware that we all have separate realities in how we see the world, and that this influences how we interrelate with each other.
- ✓ It is time to re-tune the traditional measurement tools many organisations use of a daily basis.
- ✓ **Cultural inQuiry**™ is the progressive new way to reset organisational culture by overcoming barriers that prevent organisations from implementing their plans.
- ✓ We need to **Un**learn to learn.
- ✓ Using self-reflection aids our development and greater understanding of our thinking process.
- ✓ Learning needs to be embedded as part of the organisational culture.
- ✓ Learning inspires ongoing creativity in individuals and an organisation.
- ✓ **Blockers** are a real barrier to a healthy culture and organisational performance.
- ✓ Using a **Critical Friend**® enables thinking to be challenged in a non-threatening positive way.
- ✓ When an organisation's culture is focused on co-creating a psychologically safe ecosystem, creativity flows and is enhanced. The **me** becomes **we**.
- ✓ When **me** turns to **we**, it is possible to co-create new ideas in a psychologically safe ecosystem, where our **agility ability**™ is unlimited.

Part Two goes behind these Inner Agility ideas to share more about why organisations and leaders are stuck.

We have insights, research and practical case studies for those readers that are ready for the deep dive into the transition from Inner Agility to Team Agility.

PART TWO

TEAM AGILITY

CHAPTER ELEVEN
BEHIND THE SCENES

Our research journey

Our research journeys began by revisiting all the different issues, challenges and problems leaders are facing when it comes to improving overall performance.

The next phase was to learn about the various ways leaders look to both assess and deal with the issues.

Questions we asked include:

1. How is it determined what the problem, issue or challenge really is?
2. What are the internal and external influences that impact the challenges or thinking?
3. Is this an isolated case or repetitive challenge?
4. How are the identified challenges aimed to be overcome and / or solved?

The more we investigated the organisational challenges the more it became apparent that the potential core of the issues happen due to separate realities, like how the leadership team and the team have separate realities or different perceptions about what the challenge really is.

To overcome any further misunderstandings, we decided it is possibly better to put our co-creator hat on as opposed to looking at this from a general or conventional leader perspective. We then decided to combine the above questions with how they related to building high performing teams by integrating Cultural inQuiry™.

With this new perspective as a co-creator using Cultural inQuiry, let's review the questions together.

1. By using Cultural inQuiry to determine the true source of the problem, issue or challenges within your teams - let us share what's different.

It is important to recognise here that without an understanding of going beyond what motivates people, it will be impossible to create a high performing team. The root cause of the problem is not something a leader can immediately identify without first understanding the fundamentals of the holistic human experience. Just as we shared earlier in Part One.

When the problem is left to fester because it is unclear, the misalignment between the organisational objectives and the individual contributes to deeply dysfunctional teams. This is where it is possible to see blaming, conflicts, hidden agendas, and general apathy kick in. These teams struggle to meet their targets, resulting in poor performance and unacceptable results. Our individual world view is created from our past, our culture conditioning, our circle of influence and our fluctuating state of mind. All of these forms of social and cultural conditioning influence how we can connect to each other. It is no wonder we have so many misunderstandings between ourselves.

As a co-creator the team environment elevates to a new level of performance by collecting and considering the whole teams' perspectives. By doing this we have found that there are surprising insights into issues that leaders would normally consider a mystery because they could never see them simply by reviewing performance metrics. Using Cultural inQuiry is also helpful in knowing how to overcome the misunderstandings and navigating ego flare ups that occur within yourself or your team members. Momentum of problem solving comes from integrating the non-linear aspects into one collective focus.

2. What are the internal and external influences that impact the challenges or thinking?

Our research and practical experience confirm that learning can no longer be an isolated event, changes are too rapid. What we found is that by the time a conventional training session is completed and implemented, there is already a need for something different. This is why the insight-led cycles is needed to keep high performing teams in flow, regardless of the uncertainty.

That is why a more useful culture change philosophy is one embedded within the team that focuses on co-creating and operationalising plans. As a co-creator it is possible to collaboratively develop and share information spontaneously, which enables everyone to overcome the barriers of different departments, reducing the silo effect. Knowledge needs to be accessible and transparent for everyone within the team.

As a co-creator we would collectively identify what the internal and external influences are and how these are impacting the challenge or thinking about the challenge. This approach would integrate the team's individual knowledge about how to connect meaningfully. Understanding that the whole team is on the state of mind elevator will help with co-creating a successful brainstorming session to embrace everyone's best in the moment. Using Cultural inQuiry we can collectively create a safe space to keep the team on the cycle of ongoing reflection.

3. Is this an isolated case or repetitive challenge?

What we found as co-creators is that with multiple perspectives rotating views regarding a specific challenge it would rarely be repetitive. In addition, from a co-creator viewpoint, everyone is involved in making the whole investigation inclusive. If the same person is constantly responsible for reviewing the problem, their blinkers or biases are left unchallenged, potentially making the issue vulnerable to becoming repetitive. This is another reason that ongoing team reflection is so valuable to disrupt the cycle of the same perspective only seeing the same solution. When using Cultural inQuiry it is possible to reduce barriers to collaboration.

4. How are the identified challenges aimed to be overcome and / or solved?

Co-creators collaborating towards operationalising a plan to overcome the challenge have a very high success rate. This is simply due to the effective strategy development that occurs when there is safe space for creativity to contribute to team flow. The outcomes of the potential challenges are never predetermined since they are insight-led. The insight-led cycle solves all challenges as they come up. Cultural inQuiry keeps the team on track and in flow.

For a team to improve their agility ability™ we make the following recommendations.

When evaluating existing communication channels its valuable to consider full stakeholder input to understand everyone's needs and purpose of the products or service provided to avoid any implications. Once the communication and information flow are established, it is possible to make the necessary improvements. Clearly, as co-creators, communication will flow once inner agility is acknowledged within everyone on the team. Using Cultural inQuiry provides the shift on how this process is managed, which is pivotal for a co-created implementation strategy.

Research has indicated that clear communication is at the heart of human-to-human interaction and connection. When there is miscommunication or a misunderstanding, a domino effect of problems spirals out of control. Miscommunication can end up resulting in a misalignment of expectations. The consequences of this have been severe, leading to low morale, disengagement, and lack of trust. Another symptom of unresolved misunderstandings or conflict is increased levels of people on sick leave.

The increase of people on sick leave, and poor performance due to anxiety and depression is contributing to a new trend that is emerging, called *quiet quitters*[16] or *presentism*[17]. Presentism is when the employee shows up physically but lacks engagement and only does the basic minimum to stay employed.

The OECD[18] found a jump in days absence for work due to ill health between 2010 and 2022, highlighting the impact of pressures on our personal and professional lives is real and is at an all-time high, directly impacting overall performance metrics and cost for employers.

A major influence from our perspective is that there are so many contributing factors, it is challenging to determine the true source of the problems. It is sometimes easy to miss the issues between people if there are misunderstandings that are unresolved. Having experienced it ourselves as CEOs, we understand and are not surprised, based on the multiple complexities every CEO must juggle on a day-to-day basis. A company that is filled with co-creators is more likely to be successful because it has an engaged team of people filled with intention, compassion, and loyalty. This way the majority will work towards achieving the desired co-created vision.

Managers and leaders must understand that the best way to have a positive impact on their company is to upskill towards being co-creators of high performing teams that are aligned, motivated, engaged and committed to achieving all goals.

By implementing a co-creative culture, the conventional barriers will essentially evaporate simply because now we are not forcing alignment. Alignment will be an outcome of co-creating because everyone's view and contribution are a part of the process.

We will now continue to discuss more about diversity and what it means from our perspective in the next section.

Diversity

For the purpose of this book, the definition we use for diversity is all encompassing, it includes identifying and recognising every person as a unique individual, as much as it considers a group of people sharing similar perspectives and or attributes.

For example, two people from the same village, speaking the same language, who are the same gender and age are still diverse in their world view or perceptions about life. From our perspective, once we can deeply understand how our minds work it is possible to begin to realise that each of us is experiencing a unique version of reality. In other words, no person is seeing or experiencing the world the same way as any other person.

Just like there are no two snowflakes exactly alike. This is because every individual snowflake takes on a slightly different path from the sky to the ground. Each path encounters varying atmospheric conditions that affect the shape of every snowflake making them all unique. This is similar in how our separate realities are created by our own thoughts and perceptions of the world that come from our cultural conditioning.

Diversity includes different personality types, skill sets, physicality, nationality, age, ethnicity, sex, sexual orientation, religion, political affiliation, education level, veteran status, cultural background, family composition, marital and parental status, hobbies, interests, values, and financial situation, among other things. Each member of a team must be valued and recognised for their unique characteristics. We must avoid getting tangled in the sticky web of focusing solely on our differences and perceiving these differences as a threat to us. When we connect with others from a place of calm, we realise that we don't need to stay stuck in our old ways of thinking, we can be free to respect and celebrate cultural differences by using Cultural inQuiry™.

> Diversity is multi-dimensional. It is important to appreciate and value the differences in each person. Inclusion is when we can begin to see the essence of each other and realise just how unique and similar we truly are. Everyone is original.
>
> *Dr. Cari*

Cultural identity

The term culture can also be ambiguous. It has many connotations and different interpretations, depending on who you ask and is also context specific. Countries of one's origin have what experts call National

Culture[19] and heritage. Countries have regions, different communities or cities that identify with regional culture.

Regardless, the culture or cultures where each of us grew up impacts our relationships with the greater world based on family values, eating, dressing, speaking, communication, celebrations and many more influences. There is also our generation's culture to contend with, sexual orientation, gender, family, and ethnic belonging. Even more intriguing is the professional culture, team culture, business unit culture, industry culture and organisational culture, all that make us respond to the rigours of the world in a different way.

A key finding from Dr. Cari's research[5] discovered that our individual culture can be a significant invisible barrier to communication between stakeholders. The reason is we all have multiple layers of *different cultural identities.*

From an organisational culture perspective, Dr. Jacqui's research[6,10,11,12] found organisational culture had a significant influence on change sought across an organisation and acceptance of change by individuals.

Ignoring the fact, we all have multiple cultural identities that add to the quicksand of communication difficulties within a team environment. When we are walking around on autopilot, dominated by our unconscious biases, it is easy to make assumptions about others. It is these 'assumptions' that can cause offence and create an impression that someone is not valued or respected within the team.

Normally, these labels and assumptions are from the illusion that we have to believe everything we think. Cultural inQuiry encourages teams to question their automatic judgments and assumptions. We have found that doing so improves the team's connection, flow, and agility ability.

CQ One of the findings from Dr. Cari's research[5] noted that the majority of participants believed their existing stereotypes from their cultural conditioning about another group. However, the same participants claimed they would openly meet people from that group with fresh eyes. What was an interesting finding is that if they ended up not liking the person for some reason, that they would return to believing the original stereotype is correct.

From our perspectives as scholar-practitioners this has significant implications within high performing teams. It is essential to observe and acknowledge the different unconscious bias that is operating within our personal thinking systems. For example, if someone is unaware that they are constantly seeking to validate their unconscious beliefs with confirmation bias, no shift in perspective will occur. Confirmation bias is when the person will only seek information that supports their existing views and neglect information that contradicts these views. This is why Cultural inQuiry is necessary to jolt us out of our unconscious automatic pilot.

Let's go back to the fact that most of the population all have multiple layers of culture within them or multiple cultural identities. Different cultures can still influence you even if you never leave the specific country you were born in. Also, it is important to note that living in the same country that you were born in does not make you beholden to a single culture. Those that have never left the town or the city they grew up in, through education, meeting people and experiences, can still change or increase their perspective, just as the influence of technology exposes us to many different cultures, traditions and customs can also influence our cultural identity.

Our research reinforces[5,6] that, as global business owners, we can no longer apply blanket judgements, stereotypes, or generalisations about what is and is not acceptable in a specific country's culture. Migration is disrupting the status quo, integrating multiple needs, values, and preferences within one place. Don´t get us wrong, of course there will be different laws, rules, customs and traditions within different jurisdictions or countries. What we are referring to is that the people or the population within that country will have multiple cultural identities that must be considered. Especially in co-creating glocal teams.

Incorporating Diversity, Equity, Inclusion, and Belonging (DEIB)

Diversity, Equity, Inclusion, and Belonging (DEIB) can boost productivity, innovation, and the overall cultural dynamics within an organisation. Using an employee engagement strategy that includes DEIB should be aimed at helping lay the foundations for building an inclusive workplace culture. The goal of DEIB initiatives should be focused on creating a workplace where every individual feels valued, respected, and empowered to contribute their unique perspectives and talents to the organisation's success. We have seen this work effectively in organisations and not work in others. The approach to communication across the organisation and the underlying culture has supported successful implementations of DEIB.

> Used effectively, DEIB can enhance an organisation by drawing in a cross-section of culture and experiential knowledge to provide greater depth of service capability. Our uniqueness makes that difference.
>
> *Dr. Jacqui*

CQ This reflection is supported by a Gallup survey in 2022[20]. One area shows only 33% of employees believe they have the same opportunity for advancement as everyone else in their organisation, with 21% of HR leaders believing the same.

From our perspective, once a co-creating culture is embedded it will act as the heartbeat pulsing teams into flow. The lifeline to the team is when everyone is seeking to be a co-creator as opposed to leading. This ethos brings a sense of belonging where the team is free from limiting beliefs and there is space for fresh insights. Cultural inQuiry shows us all how to communicate more authentically by accepting and acknowledging we all have unconscious and conscious bias and that is OK. This helps to navigate our emotional experience with gentle acceptance that empowers everyone towards a sense of wellbeing and belonging both at home and at work.

Our unique diversity

It is clear then that understanding the real definition of diversity is pivotal to unlocking the potential of your workforce. Your employees are individuals first and foremost, and you want to build an inclusive and psychologically safe environment that recognises their uniqueness.

Here are some common beliefs that came out of our various research with regards to communication effectiveness between people from different cultures. We invite you take time to consider each statement and see if you agree or not.

1. Current Belief: (mind-made obstacles)

Most leaders still believe that diversity or DEIB initiatives are about understanding all the cultural nuances in order to manage their teams effectively.

Is this belief still relevant? Do you agree? Disagree?

The majority of diversity, equity, inclusion and belonging (DEIB) initiatives are not having the desired impact because they still encourage an US versus THEM (Leadership team and employees) mentality, which defeats the purpose. These are strong indicators, from our perspective, that there is only a superficial understanding of the value of diverse perspectives within an organisation. This is an easy oversight to make as any type of initiative achieves better outcomes if it is co-created with other stakeholder groups.

We analysed several Diversity and Inclusion statements openly available on the internet and in specific business cases. From our perspective, many of the initiatives are still lacking depth and implementation. It is important to recognise that these statements can come across as inauthentic, tokenistic, or superficial. There is often the perception that an organisation says one thing but does another.

2. Current Belief: (cultural learning expectations)

Most leaders are investing time and energy to learn about different cultures in the hope of reducing potential friction between global team members.

Is this belief still relevant? Do you agree? Disagree?

Today's leaders must be like the conductor in an orchestra, keeping all stakeholders focused on a common goal. Research is continually proving that human-to-human conflicts are increasing and blocking performance outcomes in all areas of the organisation[21]. Knowing about different cultures does not resolve miscommunication between team members.

The biggest misunderstanding about team communication is that we tend to believe that everyone must think the same way we do personally, for us to be OK.

Team productivity and collaboration improves when they know it is not possible for everyone to agree all the time[22]. This is the way our minds are created and can experience a sense of calm when we know we know longer must try to convince others to see things the way we do. We all have our own separate reality.

CHAPTER TWELVE
THE WORKPLACE CHALLENGE

Plan implementation

All types of teams and organisations are struggling to implement their plans. There is relentless surge in everyday distractions that need constant attention. The daily challenge of keeping team members focused on delivering strategic outcomes versus surviving the complex business landscape is ongoing. Leaders continually face distractions such as the global economy, climate change, political events, and speed of technological change. The gap is about creating a sustainable culture that can endure an ecosystem of constant changes[27].

The pressure to be agile, innovative, and up to date with the latest technology is causing a chaotic approach to implementing change that is neglecting the human side of business. People are reporting unprecedented levels of anxiety, apathy, and fear about their futures[26]. The complexities and level of uncertainty continue to cause real harm and risk to the overall wellbeing of people.

Yet interestingly, when you think about it, if there are no people, there is no team, and no organisation can continue to exist.

Let's explore these issues further for a better understanding by looking at how the workplace problem historically evolved.

What is the workplace challenge? A historical 360 view

What is the workplace challenge? A surface view of the workplace could include being rigid, rule based, and process driven with a top down management structure. The popular approaches to measuring or gauging success is by assessing the numbers to confirm profitability. These performance metrics have been passed through the centuries until now.

The core leadership philosophy has always been more of command and control style. This was simply due to the structure and nature of business, especially during the industrial revolution in places such as factories. With this leadership style came a dictation of work schedules that were not flexible or adaptable to the needs of the worker, and everyone had to fit in. The strict policy and procedures controlled the expectations, behaviours, along with appropriate disciplinary guidelines. Work was informed by processes, and staff were not expected to think but act as prescribed[17]. This style of management and leadership has continued with potentially small adaptations over the decades, transferring from one generation to the next.

The employee was historically solely responsible to keep themselves motivated to show up on time, meet or exceed job expectations, be loyal and even grateful to have an employer. It is interesting now to be aware and to observe how our cultural conditioning can influence the individual views regarding different generations. People generally lived to work and take care of their families. Focusing on surviving from a financial aspect which was obviously one of the top priorities.

Communication and information sharing was and mostly remains largely as one-way, top down. Power and promotions were common goals and desires of the employees and employers alike. Some of you may remember the common phrases such as "here to be seen and not to be heard" or "don't speak until spoken to". There was or is no mechanism or possibilities for feedback where leaders could openly consult others about ***their decisions*** regarding the direction of the organisation. This would have historically been considered a weakness as a leader and may still be an active part of some leaders ongoing cultural conditioning that of course varies from person to person.

This type of organisational culture inevitably led to trust issues, conflict at the workplace catalysed by bullying and little or no recognition. The global working environment has so many different areas of complexities to manage that are affecting optimal performance[6]. The major attribute being how human-to-human interactions and connections occur[5].

Understanding that this section was a quick glance in the rear-view mirror to share why we discovered it is now time to rethink these conventional interventions. Historically, linear thinking was possible. Meaning leaders could comfortably measure and manage future risk with long term plans. Today, the current volatility means we can no longer rely on processes and systems to overcome the ongoing challenges presented. Especially, at the exhilarated pace we are currently experiencing technological advancement.

Co-creating a new perspective using Cultural inQuiry can easily help to rethink what it takes to meet these challenges head on. In doing so, we provide the retooling of current concepts and generate insights that can redefine how we work in a positive way by focusing on the people.

Workplaces today are undergoing a massive shift as companies seek to become agile and responsive to the needs of their stakeholders like employees, suppliers, and customers. The key to winning this tug of war between conventional and modern disciplines is by courageously developing our inner, team and organisational **agility ability™.** This is the key to operating in a fluid work environment that is always changing.

Companies are now increasingly seeking to engage and align their workforce to create an environment of continuous improvement and innovation. Technology has enabled the sharing of knowledge across geographical boundaries almost instantly. Allowing people to work remotely using the internet or connected networks has significantly reduced barriers of access when it comes to communication[23] and inclusion[10,11].

This has drastically transformed the workplace we have been accustomed to and has made it possible for employees to collaborate, share information and innovate. Our evolved workplace environment has improved its capacity to be fluid and dynamic, although does require a new or slightly amended structure. It is about creating an atmosphere of collaboration. It is about encouraging people to take ownership of their work and feel empowered[6,10].

This brings us to the question:

Where does this take organisations and what should be their area of key focus in this century and the next?

Boundaries have been brought down by technology, education is more accessible and flexible with migration being a common trend bringing all cultures together. People have also become more aware of their individual preferences, calling for a more inclusive team environment. Granted, a focus on deepening our understanding of effective human-to-human interaction will provide the necessary edge required for both personal and organisational growth and development. Essentially calling to advance people development with Cultural inQuiry to better understand, position, and bring out the best in the team[5].

Managing people

People are an organisation's most valuable asset, and the task of managing teams is a tricky one. By being attuned to the nuances that determine how people perceive and react to given situations, companies can hopefully encourage their team members to be more engaged.

The **LENS Framework**™, supported by **Cultural inQuiry**™, is grounded in human resilience, psychology, neuroscience, business strategy, leadership development, and communication that facilitates overcoming the complexity of managing people effectively. It is time for leaders to go beyond the functional aspects and look at the organisational structures that enable and facilitate people to do their jobs effectively. A key question is if decision makers are missing out on the many opportunities that diversity offers to its workforce.

We highly recommend that leaders seek to understand that people are not easily replaced and that there are unique characteristics in each of the employees that can be harnessed to boost connection and productivity. It is important to recognise that culture is multi-dimensional, and that people have multiple cultural identities. People are not homogenous, and they are influenced by their unique backgrounds, personalities, and experiences.

Conventional assessment tools were used to help leaders to conduct a personality[24], cultural, or behavioural analysis[25] on their team members. This was a way to categorise people based on their ethnic background, culture, language, gender, age, and many other checkpoints. Then of course there were the sub-cultures within your organisation that also needed further categorising, and on it went. It was, and in some instances still is, common to attempt to apply some type of profiling tool to understand team members better[24,25].

We have seen the range of different types of assessment tools that attempt to determine your personality so you can be categorised, identified, or labelled as a certain style so others can 'identify you and compare you to themselves'[24,25] are not overly helpful at all with high performing teams. The challenge from our perspective is that when we try to categorise and label people it can end up perpetuating our differences in a negative way and causing deeper silos. We think that we are all ready to discover new ways of creating synergy with connection between ourselves and others.

In our experience these types of profiling or assessment tools can actually have an adverse influence by creating deeper silos, reinforcing existing stereotypes, and perpetuating bias in some instances, causing microaggressions, and emphasising differences. Therefore, making their suitability questionable in today's work environment if not managed effectively. Interpretation of profiling tools is needed to educate the users and minimise the potentially negative aspects such as labelling others.

All of these factors contribute to both the cultural and social conditioning of individuals, which impacts how they communicate, behave, and relate to other people. Each of these cultural identities are original to the person concerned and cannot easily be categorised or generalised when we first see or meet or know them.

The uniqueness of every person must be valued and respected[5]. It is when we assume things about others when we first see them, thinking we know about someone based on how they look, behave, or speak that disconnection and misunderstandings start.

People in general are seeking to be accepted and desire to be treated fairly by having a voice that is truly heard. They should also feel safe in expressing themselves and they should be encouraged to do so. When people feel like they are part of a team, they are motivated to perform well and give their best[10,25].

High performing teams function best when multiple perspectives are integrated and applied. During the research inquiry process, it was discovered that long standing rules or policies do not cater for collective decision making[5]. It is often assumed that allowing for diversity is a general pass to ignore established company policies and procedures, which is not the case.

What we see in the business world is that many policies and procedures are simply outdated and need to be revised to meet the changing needs of the stakeholders, company, and society. The key is to balance the need for consistency with the need for flexibility and adaptability.

CHAPTER THIRTEEN

SOLUTION OVERLOAD OR BLIND SPOT AND ACRONYM OVERLOAD

Blind spots

Lack of awareness of team dynamics or any type of unconscious bias could be a blind spot for managers and leaders. For example, a manager or leader may unknowingly favour one team member over another. This could be from background, communication style, or other factors while they overlook the contributions of other team members. Other blind spots may be constantly playing devil's advocate or expecting all your team to work at your pace. Another possibility is neglecting the realisation that we are all vulnerable to fluctuating floors that our current state of mind elevator is on.

Organisationally, blind spots can be as simple as not fully understanding the roles and responsibilities of staff, their working style and how a leader's working style impacts the team. Such blind spots can lead to ineffective decision-making, poor team morale, lack of team diversity, and loss of productivity and business. The misunderstandings and conflicts between teams simply due to the different interpretations of policies or definition of terms. Addressing such blind spots is an enabler to co-creating a more inclusive and effective team culture, where all team members feel valued and supported.

To understand blind spots further, we invite you to take a look at the image below. What do you notice about the thought bubbles of each person?

The illustration above recognises that everyone has blind spots (even with full vision) with regards to what they experience or see, it is best explained by blindfolding team members and connecting them to an item, in this instance an elephant, to see what they believe is in front of them. The picture above also shows the variety of interpretations of their perception of reality. A perfect example of how we each have different ways we view the world, like how people believe their own view and have difficulty with understanding the circumstances of others. What this means is it is necessary to recognise the potential misunderstandings solely because we all view the world from a different perspective.

By shining a light on the blind spots, we offer top leadership a relevant and usable blueprint, an action-based roadmap, to navigate this uncertainty with clarity. It is based on the research that has contributed to Cultural inQuiry[5,6,10,11,12].

This means that the knowledge we have gained through our research as scholar-practitioners, combined with decades of practical experience, has been further developed into a unique approach to help organisations holistically get to the next level of performance.

What is a scholar-practitioner?

This is a popular question that always gets asked of us. We tend to take this for granted that everyone understands what a scholar-practitioner is and what we actually do. To provide clarity and consistency here is brief explanation:

A scholar-practitioner is someone who has a Doctorate of Business Administration (DBA). A DBA is the same as a PhD in that both are doctorates at the same level. There are, however, differences in the approach taken in contributing to knowledge.

Someone with a PhD has focused their research on contributing to existing knowledge, known as contributing to theory. They add to established theories by providing further evidence or proof that will either prove or challenge the current results. A good example is the progression of cancer treatments, building bridges or infrastructures, mining, or another being the emerging treatment of psychological disorders.

Whereas someone with a DBA has focused their contribution to knowledge on both the contribution to theory **and** the application of theory directly into practice.

In attaining our doctorates, we combined our academic learning and research findings with our extensive practical experience to develop our practice further. We are able to act as a bridge for decision makers and provide an instant link to relevant research that will be helpful in resolving their unique business challenge.

One of Dr. Cari's mentors is a Formula One fan. Using this example, you would not want anyone but the highest trained people in the pit ready to troubleshoot unexpected issues and support the driver to win the race, linking all their knowledge about the performance required to beat the competition. Immediately assessing the situation, challenging existing thinking and linking their advanced knowledge with any issues on the spot to ensure that one moment of the race is not missed.

From a differing perspective, Dr. Jacqui is working with an industry project team researching the inclusion of people with physical and mental challenges and the adaptation needed as a result in Formula One racing. This covers drivers, support teams and spectators. Findings confirm that needing adaptation to enable inclusion does not preclude participation, troubleshooting and winning. Vehicles and work environments can be adapted to keep equity in racing, it is adapted racing. It is the expected basic facilities that are missing that create challenges. Such an issue requires lateral thinking in the first instance and action thereafter. In this instance, with no elevator to the podium platform, only steep stairs, and no steps to the podium itself, the support team carried a physically challenged driver up the stairs and lifted her onto to podium to receive her trophy.

This responsiveness, being ready to research the issue and take action, adapting to the situation that arises, is what DBA scholar-practitioners do for the people within the organisation.

Note: *we have not used the words 'disability' and 'disabled' in line with the wording of various regulations and Acts. Disability as a word is no longer appropriate. People are not 'dis-abled' with no consideration, they adapt. An interview with Ellie Cole, multi-medal winning Olympic athlete, an Australian Paralympian icon, shone the light on the topic of adaptation and competing on equal grounds.*

Solution fatigue

CQ Did you know that statistics show that 91% of strategic plans are failing to be implemented?

As we have highlighted earlier, business leaders continue to be bombarded with new solutions. We found that most are essentially the traditional concepts or approaches. These processes and models are mostly wrapped up to look different. Strategy development for instance is a perfect example.

The C-suite executives are required to work collaboratively to align their efforts with the vision and team to achieve overall organisational success. Each one is accountable to uphold an organisational vision, strategic plans, governance, profitability, and performance evaluation. When any area is identified as underperforming or not meeting agreed objectives, that person responsible is often replaced in an attempt to inject a new level of inspiration.

Even if the person ends up being replaced, ultimately nothing changes. Even though an outsider or board members see a lot of action happening in the name of change, re-engineering, or leadership blind spots. A fresh way is to reconsider the core of the problem that could be invariably missed because of an innate fear of upsetting the status quo, rocking the boat or potentially introducing new problems.

Based on our research, previous experience is often mistakenly re-applied to present challenges, when the leader just unconsciously assumes the same circumstances are repeating themselves as opposed to a new inquiry to assess the current situation. We refer to this as ***automatic pilot*** or 'failing to see decision-making blind spots'. We would be inclined to further describe this phenomenon as a form of 'sleepwalking' except that you are awake.

New types of executive education continue to emerge. This includes presenting new philosophies of leadership, strategy development concepts, business process re-engineering, and projects, all focused to bring about some form of change. The external environment is also flooded with change initiatives across the PESTLE (political, economic, social, technical, legal and environmental factors) divide[17]. No sooner are we familiar with one concept, a new one develops. This really propels the challenge for everyone to keep up with new knowledge.

This is particularly common in technology. From:

- Web 1.0 - read-only - information connections, to
- Web 2.0 - participant social - people connections, to
- Web 3.0 - read, write, execute - knowledge connections, and now
- Web 4.0 - integration - intelligence connections[29].

For regulating from traditional telecommunications to digital landscape, technology has moved from:

- G1 - regulated public monies - command and control approach, through to
- G5 - collaborative regulation - inclusive dialogue and harmonising approach across sectors[30].

Even the age of generations continues, where today generations are listed as:

- Greatest (1901-1924),
- Silent (1925-1945),
- Baby-boomer (1946-1964),
- Gen X (1965-1979),
- Millennials (1980-1994),
- Gen Z (1995-2012), and now
- Alpha (2013-2025),

where the Alpha generation are connected 24/7 and only know technology[6,10].

Acronyms describing our state of affairs are also changing rapidly. We have seen:

- DEIB - diversity, equity, inclusion, belonging[31],
- ESG - environmental social governance[32],
- VUCA - volatility, uncertainty, complexity, and ambiguity[33],
- BANI - brittle, anxious, non-linear and incomprehensible[34],
- AI - artificial intelligence[35],
- Block Chain[36],
- DAO - decentralised autonomous organisation[37],
- Crypto - hidden, secret - cryptograph[38],

- Cloud Technology[39], and more.

The hidden barriers

There is an urgent need to shift gears, move from solving challenges from what is obvious to what is INVISIBLE, the true hidden barriers to modern business and personal performance.

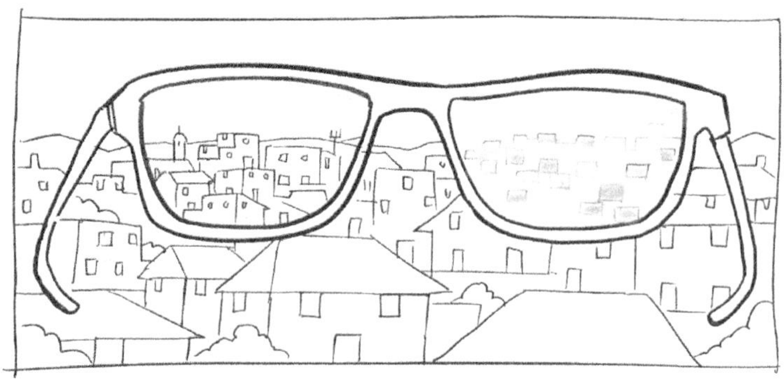

We need to make the INVISIBLE ..... VISIBLE to address it. Similar to the way we previously considered how our unconscious bias can blindly lead us away from being the best version of ourselves. It is possible to change directions and start moving through the process towards a conscious level of competence[40].

We are now in the midst of the 5th industrial revolution[41] moving from commonly known business environments such as:

- B2B - business to business,
- B2C - business to consumer, and
- B2G - business to government,

has now shifted to:

- H2H - human-to-human, and

- H2T - human-to-technology.

The real barriers of modern business and personal performance is understanding how the role of individual culture is influencing our ability to effectively communicate and acknowledge our potentially limited perception of each other. It is our own perceptions or world views that are creating misunderstandings. Each of us continues to act on *automatic pilot*, we do not question how we know what we know, what beliefs we think are true and why.

Areas to consider include:

1. Are these beliefs still working for us?
2. Is there new information that could influence and challenge our beliefs and stereotypes?
3. How are our subjective judgements and conditioned thoughts distorting our experience and influencing our world view?

Modern business success requires companies to be creative, innovative, and agile to combat uncertainty, this is a recurring point. It is no longer viable for leaders to create a strategy and be confident to predict outcomes, or projections as we have done historically. The future is unknown, in fact that starts immediately. Change is happening as you read this.

Impact on CEOs

There is increased pressure and stress on CEO's and leaders to improve performance. The blind spots of leadership continue to darken as the risk of being cancelled in this volatile corporate landscape increases. We have noticed an underlying form of panic as CEO's are blamed for the potential inefficiencies in their leadership or the failure to lead their teams to success with their visions and decisions. This type of blame and shame approach can be replaced with a different perspective when we pause and reflect. This is the potential impact of Cultural inQuiry.

As proven, changing the CEO or replacing people within the leadership team in the hope one will master the formula to navigate these new challenges could be a costly and ineffective approach.

CQ What we have discovered is that Cultural inQuiry can make a BIG difference to the team's culture with SMALL shifts in perceptions.

The ever demanding need to change something in the organisation just to be seen to make progress is common. But in the corporate world, this has led to a situation where business leaders are suffering "Solution Fatigue". By extension, solution fatigue is the repeated attempts to solve existing business problems with outdated solutions with the same traditional thinking.

We cannot solve today's problems
with yesterday's methods,
and be in business tomorrow.

Nelson Jackson

CHAPTER FOURTEEN

THE COMPLEXITY WE NEED TO NAVIGATE

Leaders and information dissemination

During the industrial revolution, a hierarchal structure was important so that information can be shared efficiently from the top decision maker to the frontline worker. During this time workers were not required to think for themselves, in general they were told what to do and any variation needed a manager's approval. If it was above the managers decision making capability or authority the decision request continued up the line until the person in charge could make the final decision.

Often, problems of a varied nature are resolved from a divisional, departmental, or functional perspective with a predetermined process or business orientation. These are often surrounded by a layer of unacknowledged decision-making biases, that can cloud clarity and sense making.

What can proceed to happen is that the main challenges afflicting the organisation remains unresolved. In today's modern business environment "change" is now the constant, ever moving. Much has been written about leading change[42] and how to be an agent of change, but change is no longer something we 'prepare for', 'adapt to' or 'resist'[43].

Innovation requires a supportive organisational culture with an infrastructure that enhances connection as a driver for human creativity. From another perspective innovation is the fuel of change driven by our **agility ability**™.

We are introducing the concept of a co-created organisation. Focusing on co-creators, appointing people who are accountable and take full responsibility of success and failures is of paramount importance. On the other hand, from a co-creator perspective, the overall goal is to have each participating team member being accountable for their part in contributing to organisational success.

For instance, a leader pivoting at the top of the organisation is critically useful in sharing knowledge. This ensures that everyone can understand the context, so that the leader can rally people towards a common vision. A CEO is the top executive who is charged with creating and sharing knowledge for a common good which could, at times, be delivered in the form of projects or training. However, there has been an unfounded belief in organisations with a traditional view that the CEO has a monopoly on the organisational knowledge. Using this knowledge to create their version of the best strategies to move into the future with. This approach is no longer viable for modern organisations who want to stay competitive and survive.

Maintaining a CEO in a traditional role and job description can result in a power distance between the leader and the led, potentially creating fear and resentment of authority if not addressed[44]. Remember earlier when we discussed ego-led leaders or the **C-EgO**™? This could be considered the fertile ground that nurtures this type of leader if left unchecked.

Other problems have arisen from this leadership model. For example:

- Ego driven micro-management and personal need or desire to try to control others.
- Restricted knowledge, flow of knowledge transfer, sharing and creation.
- Enforcement of a competitive, sabotaging, and destructive team environment based on linear structures or promotions.
- Decision making being biased and bureaucratic, leading to missed opportunities.
- Decision makers being detached from the needs of the customer and other stakeholders.
- A primary focus on profits or implementing new technology over a people focus.
- Belief that there is a complete technological solution that will eliminate people.

By traditional organisational design, decisions are centralised, authorised by a select few and then cascaded to the lower levels to be acted upon without question. The cascade flows downwards in tiers, dispersed to the workers on the frontline for execution as policy. This was a short leash type of management, and it worked very well with the absence of technology as we know it today. Although technology in this context must be seen as a channel of distributing information or instructions. Technology brings about greater efficiency, but it does not change the plan of action.

It is possible to make shifts in a hierarchical structure to easily accommodate a co-creator flow. The **CQify LENS Framework**™ can be instrumental in co-creating a culture where information is accessible, so that knowledge becomes a collective asset available to all stakeholders. One of the key competitive advantages of being a co-creator is the access to diverse perspectives and multiple sources of knowledge generation.

Workplace team engagement

Leaders are dealing with a new form of absenteeism, called presenteeism as introduced earlier.

Disengagement of team members is happening more and more as a symptom of a dysfunctional work culture. This could include a conflict with their boss, colleagues or just simply not being engaged with their work and the organisation due to their increased anxiety (either personally or professionally). Their "balloon head" keeps inflating with more and more pressures, worries and stresses. Presenteeism is harder to detect and is costing a significant amount of money and resources. The ripple effect of a disengaged worker goes out into the organisation in unpredictable ways, impacting customers, teams, and bottom-line performance metrics.

Research confirms that in some cases the workforce is disengaged due to lack of recognition[45]. We have seen different cases where the management and leadership teams are simply unable to navigate the core problem. The main problem is normally due to a form of misunderstanding or conflict between members of the organisation[5].

In different cases, management try to implement new technology that is supposed to help people communicate more efficiently. The downside we discovered is that most people were not trained how to use it properly. This actually caused more misunderstandings. The research found within those organisations the current leadership approaches are non-inclusive. This means that the leadership team does not involve the team in the decision-making process or even clearly explain how the process or technology works. We found that employees are left to figure it out on their own, creating deeper feelings of invalidation, exclusion, and increased stress.

When we start to investigate initiatives that are suffocating creativity, we discover that restrictive job descriptions, performance appraisals, disciplinary procedures, are all potentially no longer helpful. It is time for new ways to measure performance that do not involve micromanagement and static reviews by management with, at times, unacknowledged biases. It is time to shift from hierarchy to harmony using **Cultural inQuiry**™.

Employees are normally being evaluated against a set standard that does not take into account individual differences, needs or value.

Have you ever been so focused on achieving your individual KPI's that you neglect the team's goals? It is quite common to hear people panicking and making up tasks and results to look like they are on track for their KPI's the night before meeting their manager. This again is obviously not productive or good for the person, team, or organisation.

As a result, there is a minimal degree of autonomy for employees in the work environment, which can be and is counterproductive. This all contributes to the workforce feeling controlled by management and not empowered to contribute ideas, contradicting innovation as a top priority for survival. Ultimately, employees are continually expected to conform to rules and regulations that are making employee retention challenging with little trust within the team. This toxic work environment is another reason that teams stay stuck in a reaction mode when problem solving.

The biggest misstep in such organisations is their attempt to keep the traditional structures while attempting to integrate the new technologies or modern thinking. This has resulted in significant emerging problems that are deepened by working in silos, departments divided into power-driven groups, and an overall lack of accountability.

The result is stifling creativity, blocking innovation, and delaying decision making, but more crucial, enacting bad decisions. Then the pursuit of solutions begins this endless treadmill of being stuck.

Workplace complexity

The task to pivot towards a culture-based on co-creation can appear overwhelming, complex, costly, and impossible to some leaders. In our experience it really does not have to be that way. Our research-based methods make the process straight forward, stimulating, and productive. In addition, the cost of doing nothing will always carry a higher amount and risk.

Surprisingly, the first step only requires curiosity. Cultural inQuiry™ is for the progressive leader, the edge-walker that fearlessly adapts to new paradigms so that others will then follow. Fear of change explains the rise of prominent global companies collapsing in a way that is unprecedented. Those companies could have suffocated themselves with their own old-style comfort blankets of KPI's, OKR's, albeit unconsciously. Unless there is a transition in thinking with the necessary aligned implementation of plans, more will disappear.

Another variable that most CEOs and leaders are usually blind to is that performance cannot be predicted in this new landscape, regardless of historical formulas, not in the short, medium, or long term. Assumptions and dependencies that have been an ingredient in strategy development are no longer feasible[6,19,46]. This is why using Cultural inQuiry and insight led communication is game changing.

What we see as critical success factors today change by the minute and risks are evolving in a way never seen before. One can no longer intelligently guess their probability, possible frequency, and impact. Yet organisations set aside vast sums of money and resources to maintain and manage risk assessment. This could potentially be seen as a very expensive habit.

We need to question how we can shift into a new way to measure performance milestones while giving space for creativity so the team can keep flowing with ongoing change regardless of external or internal influences[6,19,58,59].

A linear or direct approach that worked for the past century is no longer viable in this unfamiliar non-linear business ecosystem.

These rapid changes require a focus on human-to-human interaction to co-create a coherent, collaborative workflow based on creativity and the **team's agility ability**.

Today, the world is getting more complex, and organisations need to surf the ongoing change to survive and thrive.

The complexities of today's world

The global population has grown phenomenally in recent decades creating new social, economic, and political dynamics. Organisations must be aware of a renewed need for a balance between the planet, profits and people[47].

Inevitably, there is a stronger need for people to collaborate and include many different perspectives in solving problems. We need to remember that each of us have different culturally conditioned definitions of what trust really means. Also, some of us tend to trust others until they prove us wrong. Conversely, others have been conditioned to withhold trust or even abuse it. As a result, genuine trust can take a long time to build up and nanoseconds to take away. Fortunately, Cultural inQuiry can significantly improve our understanding and encourage the growth of trust within teams.

Technological advancement has also made these complexities in communication and decision making more profound. As the scientific models change, people must rethink how their inner agility is subject to bias and prejudice from what they believe and perceive to be true. These complexities affect people, organisations, communities, and governments in almost the same way but on different scales.

Ultimately, research in neuroscience and resilience psychology are adding value by explaining how our minds truly work and combining this with an understanding of how this will potentially impact on our behaviour. As discussed previously, it is a common experience that uncertainty triggers increase anxiety and overwhelm within many of us. It is by using Cultural inQuiry we can begin to build our confidence regardless of the existence of uncertainty. We begin to have confidence that a new thought will bring us the wisdom we require for that moment. This is the power of insight.

Acronyms are commonly used to describe the difficult terrain and new global phenomenon people and organisations are challenged to navigate in today's world. The acronym:

VUCA (Volatility, Uncertainty, Complexity, Ambiguity)[33]

has now already been replaced and moved on by the current acronym referred to as:

BANI (Brittle, Anxious, Non-linear, Incomprehensible)[34]

BANI - a definition and application

Brittle - things appear to work on the surface but are precarious and may stop working unexpectedly at any moment.

Some people are now demanding a flexible work environment with a relatable culture and with structures that cater for co-creation. A common misconception is that processes will be accepted without engaging the team's input. Systems and processes will stop working within an organisation if there is not a consensus or buy in. When considering and evaluating existing systems, processes, or procedures it is best practice to co-create the review with all stakeholders' input. In our opinion, the misconception of not needing consultation makes it difficult for organisations to progressively manage their challenges as they are trapped in their own conditioned thinking.

What is important to realise is that these ***brittle*** processes must be underpinned by an alternative approach. This approach must support integrating fresh knowledge generated by team insights to create a seamless flow of individual and organisation performance.

Anxious - when people feel helpless and overwhelmed about decision-making as they anticipate what's next.

People are increasingly being 'absent from work', mainly due to reduced levels of connectedness, normally springing from misunderstandings, anxiety and depression[48]. Anxiety and depression can restrict our ability to be creative and responsive in the face of the unexpected changing landscapes. A priority for the leadership team is to recognise how these symptoms can influence the bottom line of the organisation. This tangible measurement could be an evaluation of overall operations, profitability, and team performance. It can be refreshing to shift perspectives to gain insight into how to improve the team's ability to connect.

Non-linear – is the opposite of being a predictable description of cause and effect change in traditional thinking or system. It is often described as complex with unknown outcomes making it challenging for control measures.

A non-linear environment is dynamic that requires businesses to be adaptable and flexible to thrive within the unknown. It can be similar to walking through a maze where you can only see so far in front of your feet and never know what comes next. Day-to-day decision making can feel risky and feel like the cause of deeper anxiety. It is part of our human nature to instinctively prefer to remain with what we know within our comfort zone. It becomes a trigger to our amygdala when things change. The real challenge therefore is our ability to adapt to the complexity by replacing fear with curiosity about the unknown of our non-linear reality. Remembering that nothing is as linear as it looks there is always a surprise waiting. BANI shows us that change is fast and furious.

Remembering that individual culture conditioning influences every person's worldview. This can be a non-linear and unexpected influence that produces unintended consequences. People are seeking to belong, connect, and create a positive impact in their lives. Cultural inQuiry seeks to regenerate an organisations capacity to co-create such impact through individual and team insights and collaboration.

Change continues as an unrelenting zig zag and requires a process that can embed these insights on an ongoing basis. This is done by inspiring a work environment that provides an experience built on a foundation of curiosity, humility, trust, respect, resilience, and accountability. Only then can people be prepared and adapt to unexpected consequences.

Once individuals find some peace with the inevitable uncertainty, fear of change reduces or even evaporates. Only then our true potential can be discovered in the space of unlimited possibilities.

Incomprehensible - as technology continues to rapidly advance along with the volatility of political and environmental conditions, people are vulnerable to being overwhelmed by unknown change. This happens while we are attempting to navigate the advancements which is past our ability to process and apply our individual understanding at this level of change.

Technology is rapidly evolving and changing our world, increasingly the speed of the changes often makes them feel incomprehensible. With the metaverse and artificial intelligence already changing the world as we know it will continue to alter how we interact and engage in cyberspace.

Clearly no one knows how this new technology will impact the future. Similarly, this will not be the last of big technology advancements. This is why it is necessary to refocus on the human aspect of connecting and working with people within an organisation or towards a common purpose. It is irrelevant if you have the best technology or the best product, your organisation is at a high risk of failure without the buy in and the agility ability of team members. We see many leaders seeking out the next big technological advancement to differentiate themselves from their competitors. Ironically, the competitive advantage comes from being a co-creator within an agile high performing team. Simply meaning that integrating Cultural inQuiry is a top priority to people first.

The world will continue to operate in a very uncertain space in the coming years. There will always be new acronyms but what we are saying is that change will always be the constant with unpredictable outcomes.

> The biggest differentiator any organisation can have is their people. The biggest differentiator in people is their current state of mind, and knowing how this can leverage their Inner Agility enables sustainable Team Abilities.
>
> *Dr. Cari*

Cultural inQuiry goes to the source of the challenge, by teaching leaders' and teams' agility ability so that they can thrive in this world of ongoing change.

CHAPTER FIFTEEN
ORGANISATIONAL CULTURE

Organisational culture and trust

We know that organisational culture is an important foundation for performance. Without a proper understanding of the culture and how it functions within an organisation, it becomes difficult to identify and address the root causes of any operational issue.

The big question becomes what foundation is required to achieve this level of performance? First, we need to investigate the company culture and dissect the priorities.

When we can evaluate high performing teams, it is common to see that there is an undisputed level of trust between individuals and there are also superior levels of communication.

Trust? Sounds simple at a first glance because the common answer or perception is that trust is a given, we trust people until we don't. Some research participants shared comments such as:

> "Of course, we all trust each other";
> "I know, we do Trust activities every year!";

> "I can never trust my manager, he is always holding information back, never open".

However, trust should never be assumed or taken for granted. Existing research confirms that 'trust' is a critical attribute that fosters communication and bridges all types of communication difficulties. Yet, what is trust? Trust in the context of relationships within the work environment is defined as believing that the other person will do what they say they would do to honour their commitments while being accountable for their actions. Trust has authenticity, logic, and empathy as drivers, where if one is breached, then trust is lost[42].

Trust between people can also be described as a form of loyalty and is important across cultures. Like other issues, trust means different things to different people. Leaders must clarify their understanding of trust to each stakeholder, as every culture perceives different meanings. Interpretations of certain characteristics in communication are assumed in different meanings assigned to them. This depends on the cultural lens applied. Individuals may also be unique in the way they perceive trust, including what it means to them and their expectations of trust.

There is, therefore, a need to develop trust building strategies or initiatives. A guideline may include setting clear goals, specific direction, communicated mindfully and with simple language that emphasises transparency and collaboration. Trust is the glue that binds intangible confidence between stakeholders, the work group and to the organisation. Trust supports authentic multicultural relationship building and is more important than political correctness, which is what most leaderships exhibit today.

Some people say it is far easier to identify what trust is **not** rather than what it is. Some say it is important to be truthful with others by not being manipulative. The challenge is that genuine **Trust** can only occur when it is associated with accountability, ethical conduct, and transparency. When this is in place it will ensure that multicultural stakeholders' relationships can flourish.

Without sufficient trust levels, parties to a conversation or discussions do not share uncomfortable perceptions of other cultures or the inherent issues that are "negative" such as "the way we do things here". Yet, these are controversial assertions as each item of concern is subject to or relative to something else.

What makes trust even more complex is that there are traits that respondents in a conversation can see and those that they can't see readily but both will affect judgement. Unconscious bias is the most profound judgement, compelling enough to require a method of awareness. That said, the process of managing unconscious personal biases relies on creating a safe environment so that it can be acknowledged.

Trust should never be assumed or taken for granted. Existing research confirms that 'trust' is a critical attribute.

What is trust?

Trust in the context of relationships within the work environment is defined as believing that the other person will do what they say they would do to honour their commitments while being accountable for their actions. Trust has authenticity, logic, and empathy as drivers, where if one is breached, then trust is lost[49].

Trust between people can also be described as a form of loyalty and in Dr. Cari's research[5], trust was rated as being highly important by all cultural groups represented.

Like other issues, trust means different things to different people. Leaders must clarify their understanding of trust to each stakeholder, as every culture perceives different meanings. Interpretations of certain characteristics in communication are assumed in different meanings assigned to them. This depends on the cultural lens applied. Individuals may also be unique in the way they perceive trust, what it means to them and their expectations of trust. A lot of our work with our clients is aimed at clarifying what trust means for them and then helping the team get clarity in how to achieve it.

We highlight the need to develop trust building guidelines, communicating mindfully and with simple language to emphasise transparency and collaboration.

It is important to be truthful with others by not being manipulative. Trust is associated with accountability, ethical conduct, and transparency to reduce the breakdown of potential relationships between stakeholders. If people do not trust each other, they simply will not feel able to share their perceptions about any type of situation. Ultimately this will lead to staff disputes, blame culture, resentment, presentism and even resignation.

What makes trust even more complex is that there are traits that respondents in a conversation can see and those that they can't see readily, but both which affect the judgements they make. Unconscious bias is something that is important to be aware of because if we ignore it, we will remain stuck in our subjective view of the world. That said, the process of managing unconscious personal biases relies on a safe environment to acknowledge individual schemas (judgements, opinions, views, and stereotypes based on our cultural conditioning).

Dr. Cari's research[5] involved 18 participants from different countries who were asked to define what trust means to them. Surprisingly there were 18 different definitions of trust. This was a huge eye opener into how their different cultures informed what trust means.

From Dr. Cari's perspective this is a very important finding that suggests we need to define what trust means to us personally and in our teams so we all can share an agreed meaning. If we do not agree collectively on a meaning this could lead to misunderstandings or internal conflict. If everyone perceives trustful actions differently than others could innocently misjudge someone as not being trustworthy[5]. For example, if we said we trust each other, but we both are unknowingly thinking it means something different it could cause conflict. Once trust is lost, it is something rarely reinstated and is very difficult to earn in the first place.

Dr. Jacqui also found that there are many different opinions about what trust[6] means. To gain a consensus from all staff members about what trust is, including how it is gained and lost is essential in any work environment. One government area she worked with, established hybrid working conditions where staff worked a combination of remote and in-office. There were various electronic monitoring and check-in parameters agreed. Staff were aware of the monitoring and expectations, based on a 'you abuse it, you lose it' agreement. Meaning that if anyone abused the trust of the management the remote working agreement would no longer be allowed. Some staff tested the waters only to find the work agreement rescinded and were required to only work in the office. New recruits went through their probationary period in the office until agreed trust parameters were established and enacted. When a clear definition and expectations are agreed by everyone it can improve the overall understanding and reduce potential conflicts.

As you can see from the above example this creates an US versus THEM scenario. This is a more conventional management style that is using fear to manage by taking away a privilege to enforce rule compliance and avoid a 'free for all' approach.

If we used a co-creative team ethos here, this could overcome both the resistance of the dictated rules or the natural human temptation to push the boundaries.

When co-creators use Cultural inQuiry, trust is reciprocal in all directions, and it is possible to flow from hierarchy to harmony.

This invisible golden thread to empowering relationships must take a formal place when we consider building high performing teams for a culture-based organisational performance measurement. In the absence of trust, it is impossible to authentically communicate as people tend to become more 'guarded' looking for the 'hidden agendas' and trying to 'protect their own interests'.

On the other hand, when we can create a trusting environment, it is important to understand the positive impact this has on the functionality of the organisation holistically. The figure below is an illustration of how these issues are modelled and what the implications on where they are situated means, both at the content and context level, visible and invisible respectively.

It is important to understand how teams can nurture a trust building environment. Trust goes beyond just within the team and extends out to how customers and external stakeholders perceive your brand. Do they trust your organisation and product/service development?

Communication

Now that the value of trust is established, the next aspect of high performing teams is communication. Some experts even go into further classifications such as saying 'diverse communication' or 'intercultural communication'. From our perspective, when another human being is speaking or interacting with any other human being, it is always both diverse and intercultural communication. People tend to ignore that even when you are from the same family, there is still diverse and intercultural communication at play. Every person has a different world view based on how they perceive and interpret their environments and/or experiences.

Case Study: In an engagement Dr. Jacqui had on understanding the higher than industry standard turnover, independent interviews were undertaken with staff who had exited the organisation. From a verbatim perspective, people provided the following reasons for leaving their job: don't like their boss, don't like someone on their team, too much pressure, lack of opportunities for learning or advancement, being under compensated, and so on.

When we dug deeper, we identified that many of the underlying issues had a basis of the lack of human-to-human connection, creating some form of interference during communication.

Communication breakdown as a form of interference

A breakdown in communication is normally based on a misunderstanding, as we have highlighted previously and in the case study above. We discuss misunderstandings a lot as it is one of the core issues in our business and personal lives. A misunderstanding occurs when the intended message that someone shares is perceived differently than it was intended. This is due to our unconscious cultural conditioning as well as not knowing and deeply understanding that we all have separate realities. Don't worry if you are still struggling to fully understand the concept of separate realities. We know it will be something new to most people.

What is important to know as a business leader is that the outcome of misunderstandings can result in various actions. This could be described as: quiet quitting, actual quitting, conflict, exclusion, and so on.

Case study: Dr. Cari offers an insight on barriers to communication. During the research process when she was investigating an organisation in Europe, she discovered that the root of all issues, challenges or problems were based on ineffective communication[5]. The organisation provides value to the existing members through sharing knowledge and collaborating industry specific strategies to achieve clients' needs, although the barriers of communication were suffocating desired objectives.

All members of this organisation represented different European countries, where English is only used as a second or third language. It quickly became apparent how important language is and how this could be a contributing barrier to communication.

For the effective flow of sharing information between members and clients, communication is a fundamental aspect. In addition to the members' capabilities of understanding English, every diverse cultural lens provides a different interpretation of common terms such as trust, promptness of responses, and client management that are currently causing misunderstandings. Our role as a co-creator is to help identify barriers to communication. This was done through a collaborative investigation with participants. A collective understanding gained insight into how everyone perceived the organisational benefits, and their individual experiences and perceptions of the meetings differently.

Poor communication is very common, and it happens at all levels of an organisation regardless of whether the structure is lateral, horizontal or in a matrix arrangement. Any time one person is communicating with another person there is a high risk of misunderstanding. The scary part is that the majority of misunderstandings that happen are never noticed. Instead, people generally think, 'hmmm I wonder why I didn't hear back from that potential client' or 'I wonder why so and so gave their notice, I thought they were really happy working here' or even 'my boss is such a jerk, I can't believe he expects me to work overtime without additional pay'. As you can imagine, the list can go on and on.

In the current business environment, it is commonly observed that:

If anyone begins expressing dissatisfaction in their working environment it can often be frowned upon. The managers' have so many different responsibilities that could delay their response times, which are all part of the invisible operating rules of the organisation's accepted culture. This can also manifest at board level who have to deal with complaints and internal conflicts, poor performance or concerns about behaviour.

There can be a sense of apathy with an unspoken assumption that the person's needs or issues are not a priority. The risks are if the employee's expectations are not met, the people involved become disgruntled and perceive other members mistakenly as uncaring, causing even further internal conflict. This spiral can grow larger and larger, if ignored.

Communication, specifically having a successful dialogue between people is certainly complex on its own. In addition to selecting the appropriate words and body language, we need to consider that everyone has different ways of interpreting the world. We suggest that this knowledge should be considered when one person delivers information or instructions to another person.

Thinking Scenario
Mark

Mark had a lovely insight whilst reading this book. He was having a conversation with his wife who had had a difficult discussion at work with a challenging colleague. She started to tell him about it and became very tearful. He saw that she was really suffering from feeling her thinking and had definitely got some basement thinking going on.

He was able to deeply listen to her without too much judgement and then made her dinner. He said he found it helpful to be able to see that deeply listening is often the kindest thing you can do when someone is in the basement of their state of mind elevator.

Then when she had felt calmer, he started to explain what basement thinking was and remind her that her state of mind elevator would rise again. He knew she would be able to see things in a clearer light and have fresh insights when it did.

One of the lovely things about explaining these ideas is when we hear that people are sharing this to support their families and friends...

We all take for granted that actually every person has a different perception of what they hear and not necessarily listening to what is really being said. This can also be dependent on their current state of mind and what is distracting them. Then when we add the deepening complexities of our individual cultural identities into the equation, one can only empathise with how easy it is to have innocent misunderstandings.

When we speak to others, it is common to assume that they share the same definition or meaning of the phrases we are using.

For example, a boss said to her key employee: "I am so happy you are here today. I need extra help on a specific client case I know you will excel at, but we will need to stay until we are finished to meet this urgent deadline".

Initially, this could be like a compliment. Ironically, the employee actually quit on the spot. She shared her perception that the boss always picked on her for extra help because she never expected any additional pay, was too scared to ask, always seeking extra validation that she was good enough, and she was tired of being taken advantage of.

As you can see the boss thought it was a nice gesture to recognise the quality of the key employee's work and instead it was perceived as offensive. Clearly, people have different perceptions of words and actions, based on their personal cultural lens formed during their personal and business life experiences. In this sense they both experience the dialogue through the Lens of their separate reality. It may be surprising to learn that misunderstandings have a significant impact on many aspects of business. In most cases, never acknowledged by either party involved. We just assume we know why a relationship ended or maybe don't even notice that we have innocently offended someone.

The majority of leaders misinterpret this as 'not being a good listener'. Yes, we do agree that most people could improve their listening skills overall. We also acknowledge this is understandably difficult, considering the demands on our time combined with all the added pressures, stress, and distractions.

However, effective communication also goes beyond just being a good listener. For example, if you are the most active and attentive listener it still doesn't influence how we are filtering the information through our own worldview. We need to explore the true source of such misunderstandings.

Case study: Dr. Cari offers a few thoughts on evidence-based insights: 'During my ongoing research[5] it became apparent that a barrier to implement the plans agreed by the board was because of the difference in views on what is considered an acceptable response time to an email. To some, a prompt response means some form of acknowledgement of receipt of the inquiry within a specified time, normally within hours or on the same day. Others considered any delays are interpreted as not caring or unprofessional. Without clarification that provides a mutual consensus on meanings that define behaviour and actions can cause many problems.'

One problem could be a feeling of one person being more important than another. This discrepancy means there is a fundamental problem which can be viewed from a cultural perspective, in that one is perceived as being superior to another. This can all spiral off in our minds very quickly into creating a situation that did not even exist or was even intended in the first place. We can often resolve these misunderstandings simply by considering another person's perspective and asking for clarification. It can be surprising how people can misinterpret someone's actions or words and how a quick check in can unite the team again.

Microaggressions - barriers to communication within teams

Communication barriers can sometimes be invisible and happen in the form of an intentional or unintentional action, comment or question that could be perceived as offensive by another. This is referred to as a microaggression. Training about microaggressions can be helpful to bring awareness to people about the potential harmful effects and consequences if left unresolved. However, in our experience, without proper context and follow-up sessions, this type of training can potentially cause more harm than good.

When people become aware of certain phrases or questions that are classified as microaggressions and continue to use them, it can contribute to a culture of suffering, blame and exclusion. When we know how to overcome the situation peacefully and responsively, that can initiate a learning opportunity to build trust and connection. Diversity is based on the understanding that even though we all have unique world views based on our cultural impressions, we are in fact all human beings.

But the most important aspect of resolving and overcoming microaggressions within teams is embedding and aligning an ethos that is embracing diversity naturally, not just as a superficial or tokenistic initiative. Using **Cultural inQuiry**™ it is possible to create awareness about microaggressions combined with a focus on how to be responsive in these situations with mutual respect.

CHAPTER SIXTEEN
TOXIC WORKPLACES

What we know for sure is that the potential 'symptoms' of a toxic workplace culture could come out as boardroom bullying, quiet quitting, increased absenteeism or presentism, conflicts leading to tribunals, loss of revenue or acquisition apathy to name a few. So, let's explore these topics at a high level to share more context about what they mean and how they affect an organisation.

Boardroom bully

When there is a lack of trust and poor communication between executives, the board can be called dysfunctional. C-suite (CEO, CFO, COO, etc) executives have commonly shared that they can feel at times like others are trying to dominate or manipulate them. This can lead to feeling more vulnerable to the pressure of agreeing with the majority in order to 'belong', be accepted or included in the group, all for 'job security'.

This is what we refer to as an ego dominated leadership that utilises the illusion of power to instil fear tactics to maintain control and keep perceived power over people that work within their organisation. Ego dominated leadership tactics also contribute to 'groupthink'. This is where people tend to agree with the majority for fear of being cancelled, fired, or excluded. The board is then at risk of losing major opportunity costs when all perspectives are not heard because members do not share their true thinking.

Dr. Cari reflects: ‘Last year I was meeting with an executive who shared that because she went against a vote on a certain strategy direction she was immediately dismissed from the board. She couldn’t believe this happened after serving four successful years previously. After her dismissal the remaining board members voted to continue on with their desired strategy direction without any other further resistance. This is a type of boardroom bullying that I have heard many times when executives share their stories with me. I am always curious about why some leaders feel using this type of intimidation to instil fear within their executive team will be helpful to the overall organisation’s performance? In reality, it is only suffocating the creativity needed to be agile’.

Our research indicates the possibility of shifting leaders toward developing as co-creators to reduce these barriers using Cultural inQuiry™.

Dr. Jacqui shares how one of her clients also experienced something similar: They had been in the situation where they needed to raise the concern of evident bullying tactics only to be advised that their services were no longer required. The person who was using the bullying tactics is still employed in the role and no one has challenged her since. The organisation is not moving forward at the potential rate it could do with a more open and collaborative, co-creational approach.

Our research has shown that this type of archaic style of leadership is not effective and no longer tolerable in today’s environment.

Boards range from extremely effective through to dysfunctional. For those where there is boardroom dysfunction and/or bullying, executives are repeatedly trapped in a toxic cycle. This needs to change. Have you ever wondered what would happen if everyone was free to share their perspectives with respect and trust as the foundation of their interactions? How would that alone transform decision making and board productivity?

Changing the tide of meetings to greater creativity

Taking the first step at organisational level and using a pun of words, Cultural inQuiry encourages turning 'BORED' meetings into highly creative and even fun sessions :)

We experienced that by increasing the fun factor into teams swiftly changes the gears from neutral or non-performing to high performing. A psychologically safe environment is needed as a foundation to allow the expression of our individualism without being impeded.

Sometimes we wonder, when did we start taking ourselves and others so seriously?

Teams that have fun together - are more creative and connected. They are also more productive and inclusive[50].

Case study: Dr. Jacqui found a team who worked in an office together prior to Covid had to move to home offices during Covid lockdown to continue working. They then engaged on a regular basis throughout Covid. They created a psychologically safe work environment with twice daily check ins and light-hearted banter before moving onto work requirements and progress. The twice daily initial audio video engagement, moved to daily, then three times per week.

By taking genuine interest in each other's 'life', team members got to meet the family, see children and pets grow, and life happenings, all within the parameters of what each were happy to share.

The connectedness has continued post-Covid, even as members of the group move to different roles, organisations, and retiring. Genuine interest continues, with creativity in contributions to work practices, project delivery and the day-to-day activities of the 'team'.

As a group, for those still in the original organisation, productivity remains higher than other siloed groups, the inclusiveness is evident, and networks expanded.

By not taking ourselves so seriously, we are better engaged, more productive and inclusive as a team and individually, increasing our inner and team agility.

Dr. Jacqui

CHAPTER SEVENTEEN
ACQUISITION APATHY

Over 95% of companies use acquisitions and mergers as a growth strategy.

Over 90% of acquisitions fail. WOW!

The big question is why is this failure rate so high?

Companies that are looking for a quick way to grow often consider acquiring or merging with one that has attractive technology in place or different processes or clients that could be helpful in gaining market share.

Once the potential company is identified, the process of due diligence begins. Merger and Acquisition (M&A) specialists begin by analysing figures, merits of technology, synergies of processes, potential alignment of systems, and so on.

What our research and experience discovered is that the people within the teams were often being overlooked and neglected.

The people involved have the most impact on the success or failure of the acquisition or merger, so must be prioritised to the centre of the whole transaction. In our experience, when Cultural inQuiry™ is in action even more opportunities and benefits are uncovered during this process simply by using a different lens to view the big picture.

Research suggests that communication between all stakeholders is vital for a successful transaction[51], yet the recurring pattern of misunderstandings prevails.

In our research we identified how the role of individual culture combined with the existing organisational culture is rarely analysed, which is a terminal oversight. A fundamental ingredient of a successful acquisition and merger involves the co-creation of a new culture.

Case study: Dr. Cari offers a few thoughts on acquisition apathy: 'During 2022, I was involved in an acquisition that had eight stakeholders, all based in different countries. We would have zoom meetings to discuss the legal terms of the transaction with legal representatives that all had different expert opinions based on the country where they worked, which is acceptable. Although, in these circumstances where we are seeking to gain a consensus the diverse perspectives and personal biases became a barrier. The deal was losing traction as one side did not agree or understand the other side's points which became argumentative. Each stakeholder had a different agenda guided by the client combined with conflicting laws of their countries.

When I was contacted to help facilitate the deal the first thing, I did was to clarify the purpose and benefits to all stakeholders to keep the motivation to continue. We all agreed on the desired outcome. The next thing was to take all the legal contracts and create a fresh one that integrated all views using very clear wording, as English was a second language to most of the stakeholders.'

'Using Cultural inQuiry, which encourages humility, curiosity and empathy balanced with complete transparency every stakeholder started to show less resistance and more accountability. The challenge was ongoing as every interaction brought a new misunderstanding that required the ongoing navigation to guide each stakeholder towards new possibilities and collaboration.

Cultural inQuiry provided the space for individual stakeholders to reflect and discuss their perceptions and expectations to co-create a course of next steps. With every stakeholder having their own individual cultural lens it definitely made communication more challenging, especially with a lack of cultural awareness and willingness to connect. The outcome of this transaction was the successful completion with very satisfied stakeholders.'

The issues above are essentially symptoms rooted in poor communication fuelled by lack of / or low trust within the team members normally due to fear of the unknown or differences of other people. Gaining clarity for conscious and meaningful communication requires our willingness to reflect and acknowledge our own schema and to make space for alternative views.

Poor communication goes deeper than the surface of the problem. Prescriptive techniques and skills such as active listening, negotiation, leadership, or sales training miss out on resolving the source of the issues. It is important to say here that ANY type of skills training is always helpful, although there is something more required to go to the next level. The case study shares a great example of how insight-based communication using **Cultural inQuiry**™ achieved the desired results.

Knowing the importance of being an effective and clear communicator is essential. There has been an evolution of techniques and intelligence frameworks to aid in improving our skills. The next section takes you on how the intelligence frameworks have evolved.

CHAPTER EIGHTEEN
THE INTELLIGENCE JOURNEY - some helpful background

IQ to EQ to Cultural Intelligence to one step further towards: Cultural InQuiry™

Our rapidly evolving world requires a comprehensive approach to intelligence that includes cognitive, emotional, and cultural dimensions. As you know, we are living and working in a diverse and complex environment. This involves a holistic and practical intelligence that includes integrating Cultural inQuiry™ to upskill our agility ability™.

The evolution from IQ (Intelligence Quotient), EQ (Emotional Quotient), and CQ (Cultural Quotient) reflects how society is recognising the value of combining different forms of intelligence. The concept of IQ has a very long history dating back to the early part of the twentieth century. It was developed by two psychologists who were looking to create a test that would help them identify people who might be more likely to succeed at work.[52] It became widely accepted as a way to measure cognitive intelligence that includes skills requiring a form of logic such as problem solving and mathematics.

Eventually, as time moved on, it was discovered that it was important to understand the emotional and interpersonal skill level of a person.

EQ was introduced by Dr. Daniel Goleman who wanted to help people improve how they understood and managed their emotions[53]. EQ involves emotional awareness, self-regulation, and effective interpersonal skill development. This type of training is widely used to improve leadership and teamwork by introducing aspects around empathy and overall emotional intelligence. These skills contributed to forming more servant and empathetic leaders. Both IQ and EQ is a valuable combination that will improve our ability for tasks that are more analytical while also helping us with our interpersonal relationships. IQ and EQ together have provided a different perspective when improving communication and performance management.

As globalisation and cultural diversity in the workplace increased it became obvious that people needed skills beyond both IQ and EQ. People are connecting within a glocal environment which requires increased cross-cultural interactions that needed to be conducted more effectively. In around 2003, Christopher Earley introduced the concept of Cultural Intelligence or Quotient (CQ), which aims to improve our ability to effectively navigate and adapt to business or social situations with people from different cultures[54]. Cultural intelligence is an innovation in the field of communication that facilitates cross-cultural effectiveness.

The results of using cultural intelligence methods have been proven to be more effective than other traditional forms of communication in a global environment. The complication we discovered is that there are so many different layers of individual bias, and the tendency is for people to remain in their own comfort zone. This barrier is really limiting or even preventing the full benefit of cultural intelligence training.

We also have experienced a general misunderstanding about what it means to different people to be considered culturally intelligent.

Case study: One of our clients had a recent meeting with a person based in a different country than they were. This is a very common daily occurrence as they communicate regularly with their team members located around the world.

The two parties had a misunderstanding based on their separate realities of how an interaction should be conducted. The one person accused the other of not 'being culturally intelligent' simply because they didn't understand how business was conducted in 'their country'. Being culturally intelligent does not mean that a person is a master of knowing all the different traditions, customs, and ways of countries around the world.

From our perspective, it means that you are willing to show up and redefine new agreeable ways of engagement that are specific and suitable to the goal of the conversation. This reluctance to engage with curiosity to explore a mutually acceptable way of communicating resulted in an unresolved misunderstanding. This person did not recognise that it was happening due to their ego flare up because they believed their way of doing business is better than another's.

Based on our research, we discovered that it is even more difficult to really improve cross cultural communication without considering our cultural conditioning. Which is confirmed in the example above. The outcome of that conversation could have been completely different if the person was less judgemental of the other and was willing to expand their perceptions by improving their inner agility ability.

It is an ongoing challenge for people to recognise the influence and impact that our automatic cultural conditioning has on our perceptions of how things should be. We eagerly wanted to find a way forward to reduce these types of unnecessary misunderstandings.

Recognising this gap between cultural intelligence and the human experience, we began to explore a more holistic and practical form of inquiry. We found that Cultural inQuiry™ encourages people to deeply understand how the human experience is created to help acknowledge their cultural conditioning. This type of inquiry can achieve an improved level of inner agility. Cultural inQuiry changes conversations to meet the demands of modern business that is experiencing complexity and an uncertain business environment.

Invisible barriers

To explain further, there is a new lens that needs to be added for a deeper understanding of how our minds work. These insights will start creating true sustainable shifts that will authentically impact high performing teams and organisational growth. This is a new paradigm of inquiry that is the missing link that can decode potential misunderstandings which happen unknowingly because of what we call ***invisible barriers.***

Keeping in mind that everything we have learned to date is always helpful in moving towards the next level.

Evidence based insights

The evidence shows that in some cases the challenge identified by leaders is not always the most significant issue.

What we think is the challenge we are dealing with - is never the actual one we need to solve.

Dr. Cari

Case Study: Dr. Cari shares: 'When I first started my research inquiry into a European organisation in 2018[5], it was shared by the leadership team that they were concerned about the lack of engagement from their members. After a deep dive into the stakeholders' perspectives, it was revealed that there was a core misunderstanding about one of the services the organisation offered. This was because of the participants' different cultural views. The leadership team and the other stakeholders also shared that they had never considered how our individual cultural lens can be a barrier to effective communication between stakeholders.'

Conducting a deep Cultural inQuiry™ into the stakeholders of an organisation can produce important insights and understandings that will help to discover the real concerns. This discovery process is the first step to gaining a 360-degree view of the challenges faced so that they can be resolved to improve momentum in achieving the overall performance objectives. Sustainable Performance Metrics is therefore a tangible measurement of intangibles.

Co-creators require creativity with a tinge of imagination for innovation to happen. It requires that the majority of the team brings their "A" game to work combined with an awareness of the size of their balloon head or what floor they are on in the mood / state of mind elevator. It starts by inviting them to share their reality in the prevailing circumstances in an environment where they can openly say what they see as the problem, so that a plan to address the problem can then be co-created.

From this perspective, employees are critical stakeholders within the organisation that inspires a win-win initiative. This is how optimal engagement is co-created. This is achieved by encouraging a sense of shared ownership and accountability.

This depends on how the leadership team integrates themselves within their teams. It is based on an appreciation and recognition of individuals' preferences. It's a deeper understanding and appreciation for everyone's uniqueness.

Co-creators understand that collectively they will have an answer to the most challenging problems that they face but only when the team develops their agility and ability to be truly inclusive. Executed well, this can propel decision making, problem solving and performance to another level. As well as ensuring sustainability amid rapid change and disruptions.

Using Cultural inQuiry™ should make organisations more attractive and effective to all stakeholders. With alignment comes open communication, trust, a sense of belonging, purpose, increased engagement, attraction, retention, and autonomy with accountability.

We aim to dismantle an "**us** versus **them**" culture, meaning the leadership team versus the employees. **Culture-based performance requires we embed a new ethos that turns ME into WE.**

CHAPTER NINETEEN
EXPANDING ON Cultural inQuiry™

We have covered how Cultural inQuiry™ is a new form of inquiry into our own cultural identities that will improve our inner agility ability™ to effectively communicate and deeply connect with others. It begins by understanding how our own individual schemas are created by varying cultural influences. Then expands into how to co-create the team's agility for culture-based performance. Cultural inQuiry introduces a new paradigm for co-creating collective power towards next level organisational performance.

Many of us are still using our culturally conditioned stereotypes as an automatic reaction when we meet a person from a specific country or group. What we need to realise is that cultural stereotypes are inaccurate, unhelpful, and potentially harmful. It is helpful to remember that it is impossible to use stereotypes to assume any characteristic of a person you meet from any culture.

Historically, it was common to assume a group of people from a specific culture behaved in a certain way or shared similar traits. When any person begins to understand Cultural inQuiry deeply, they will be able to realise that it is unhelpful to be applying outdated stereotypes to others. It is unhelpful because stereotypes are always based on an intrinsically limited cultural conditioning and a biased perspective.

The ethnic and cultural identities we possess individually should be cherished and universally accepted by understanding that every person has a unique combination of various cultural influences.

Cultural inQuiry promotes curiosity when engaging with others to expand our awareness past our automatic assumptions to know the individual person we are connecting with. We are all citizens of the world or what we call 'glocal citizens'. This means we are local to where we live, and we bring all our visible and invisible cultural identities with us.

We need to be explorers with a fresh sense of curiosity about each person we meet with and not be overrun by our automatic stereotypical judgments. Understanding this alone will change the conversation around creating an inclusive world. By using Cultural inQuiry, we can begin to understand that it is impossible and fundamentally unhelpful to continue to believe historic cultural stereotypes and prejudice. This is because people can no longer be categorised just by differences without potentially false assumptions being made.

Using Cultural inQuiry, we greet each other with a new openness to learn about the person, going past our initial stereotypes and judgments. We can then effectively understand the impact of cultural influences on our human experience and relationships. It combines a useful opportunity for reflection about how our individual cultural lens contributes to our worldview.

It's a new foundational understanding that we all have separate worldviews based on our own unique combination of cultural identities. This is true for us all as human beings. This is what keeps life interesting from our perspective, it allows us to value the beauty in our differences while also acknowledging what connects us. We are connected by the fact that we all have the same human operating system. Our thoughts create our feelings about what we are experiencing, and that knowledge alone can change the world.

How Cultural inQuiry™ can improve Environmental Social Governance (ESG) strategy implementation

Environmental, social and governance (ESG), also known as Environmental Social Governance, is a broad term that refers to the ways in which organisations manage their impact on their surrounding environment. The majority of ESG strategies commonly overlook how the role of how culture is impacting the design and implementation success. Here, we are referring to all types of culture such as individual culture, the culture of organisations, regulatory bodies, governments, countries and so on. We strongly recommend that when implementing and designing an ESG plan, our culture in all contexts should be integrated with Cultural inQuiry.

The advantage of using **Cultural inQuiry**™ is to help all stakeholders understand, acknowledge, and overcome their blind spots or unconscious social conditioning. Co-creation that links ESG intentions with stakeholder needs is the missing ingredient to ensuring a sustainable impact. This is because many areas of developing the plan involve multiple stakeholders across many different countries that are all vulnerable to their different cultural conditioning.

ESG is important because it gives investors and other stakeholders a way to assess how good an organisation is at managing its impact on the environment and society. Cultural inQuiry will help your plan overcome the risks of losing customers, investors, and employees simply with clear communication.

One of the many barriers to implementing an ESG strategy is the general lack of understanding about how it affects the organisation's bottom line. Many organisations are still unaware of how much money they can genuinely **save** and the value that can be created for all stakeholders by implementing an ESG strategy. This misunderstanding makes it difficult for them to justify spending time and money on this type of project.

It is detrimental to all types of organisations that either do not have an ESG plan or that have one that is failing. It is easy to see what happens when it goes wrong, but we will share how you can get it right.

First, we would like to share our definition of what ESG is to put us all on the same page with a mutual understanding.

ESG, or Environment Social Governance, is the set of practices that organisations use in order to ensure they are operating at their highest level of social responsibility. ESG covers many areas, but it primarily focuses on environmental concerns and worker safety. In this section, we'll discuss how ESG can be integrated into your business model and why it's important.

What is ESG or Environment Social Governance?

The term ESG, or "Environment Social Governance", is a catch-all phrase that encompasses the many ways an organisation can be responsible to its stakeholders such as customers, employees, suppliers, investors, communities, and any other beneficiary of the organisation's offerings. It's one of the most important ways an organisation can demonstrate its corporate social responsibility (CSR).

Although there are many ways to define ESG, it's generally understood to include three main pillars:

1. Environmental Impact,
2. Social Impact, and
3. Governance.

Environmental Impact includes anything related to how an organisation impacts its environment from greenhouse gas emissions to waste management.

Social Impact refers to how an organisation treats its employees and customers, as well as how it interacts with local communities and governments.

Governance refers to all aspects of how an organisation is governed internally, including board composition, executive compensation policies and more.

ESG is a set of practices that organisations use to evaluate their activities with the environment and social issues in focus. They are designed to help organisations make decisions that will benefit their bottom line while also being socially responsible.

For example, an organisation might use ESG practices to make sure they're not polluting the air or water near their factory, and that they're using sustainable materials. Or they might use ESG practices to ensure that their employees are treated fairly and paid well. We believe that using Cultural inQuiry™ is an essential aspect of ESG strategies. First, it improves the employee experience while simultaneously nurturing stakeholder relationships. Secondly, it improves communication with connection that promotes wellbeing and community compassion. In addition, it is helpful with connecting all stakeholders helping overall accountability of implementation and reporting.

It is important to remember that ESG is often used as an ethical obligation by consumers who want to support organisations who take social responsibility seriously and appreciate supply chain transparency.

Potential outcomes of an ESG strategy

The potential outcomes of an ESG strategy are many and diverse. One of the most obvious outcomes is that a company will have a better reputation, which can be hard to quantify but makes a big difference in the long run. Another outcome is that they will have better relationships with their stakeholders.

The key outcome is that they will have more satisfied employees and customers, who are more likely to make recommendations about their products or services to other people. Finally, they will be able to attract more customers by prioritising doing good things for society as well as being profitable by selling products and services.

The key advantages of ESG strategy implementation are:

1. It can help you to improve your risk management, compliance, and reputation.
2. It can increase the value of your company in the long term and reduce costs in the short term.
3. It can make employees feel more engaged and give them a sense of purpose by aligning with their values and interests.
4. It can help you attract and retain great employees who want to feel good about where they work as well as make a difference in the world around them.

The co-creators' collective perspective is that full implementation of your plans requires collaboration towards clearly defined actions. To gain a clear roadmap for implementation, diverse perspectives must be synergised into an actionable direction. This process requires Cultural inQuiry™ to overcome the mental barriers and biases embedded within the decision-making process at an individual level.

Implementing your ESG plans

It is essential that the value and vision of the ESG plan has the support of the stakeholders. By using Cultural inQuiry, it is possible to weave this initiative seamlessly into the culture of any organisation. One of the main barriers to successfully implementing ESG plans is due to lack of clear goals, transparency, and poor internal / external communication. What we are discovering is that any type of initiative such as DEIB, or ESG cannot be managed within a separate department with an isolated team.

As a collective team effort during the initial planning phase, it is essential to identify key risk points and consider how the organisational culture merges within each local culture to discover potential barriers. The cultural barriers are often invisible and prevent the implementation.

There is normally minimal consideration of how to navigate cross cultural adaptability, awareness, social priorities, and regulatory processes or environments. Using Cultural inQuiry helps the engagement of all the key stakeholders by collecting and communicating their input and ideas.

ESG strategies are dynamic and will grow and change as your team and organisation do which requires individual, team and organisational agility. The implementation team must be accountable for ongoing assessment, reflection, and reporting about the impact. Measurement and milestones are key to adapting to the ongoing changes to ensure the initiatives remain relevant and sustainable. What we are discovering is how important the ESG strategy is in business and investment decision making. This means that opportunities could be lost if you do not have effective ESG plan.

Timing is everything, as new pressures are evolving every day for more organisations to be able to share the status of their plans openly.

Let's continue this learning journey in Part Three.

CQ KEY INSIGHTS OF PART TWO

In summary, the key insights, or takeaways from Part Two include:

- ✓ There is a myriad of reasons for an issue or problem to arise, many are based on miscommunication and misunderstanding.
- ✓ Diversity embraces every person's unique attributes - it is multi-dimensional.
- ✓ Each member of a team must be valued and recognised for their unique characteristics.

- ✓ Constant distractions in an ever-increasingly complex world are affecting the ability to stay focused on creating a co-creation ecosystem for the team due to competing priorities.
- ✓ People are an organisation's most valuable asset.
- ✓ By being attuned to the nuances that determine how people perceive and react to given situations, companies can make their team members more engaged.
- ✓ The **LENS Framework**™ supported by **Cultural inQuiry**™ is grounded in human resilience, psychology, neuroscience, business strategy, leadership development, and communication in aid of overcoming the complexity of managing people effectively.
- ✓ Lack of awareness of team dynamics or an unconscious bias could be a blind spot for managers and leaders.
- ✓ Disengagement of team members is a symptom of a dysfunctional work culture.
- ✓ Organisational culture is an important foundation for performance.
- ✓ Trust should never be assumed or taken for granted.
- ✓ The majority of ESG strategies commonly overlook how the role of how culture is impacting the design and implementation success.
- ✓ A breakdown in communication is normally based on a misunderstanding.
- ✓ Symptoms of a toxic workplace culture could come out as boardroom bullying, quiet quitting, increased absenteeism or presentism, conflicts leading to tribunals, loss of revenue or acquisition apathy.
- ✓ Ego dominated leadership tactics contribute to 'groupthink'.
- ✓ Culture-based performance requires we embed a new ethos that turns **ME** into **WE**.

- ✓ Cultural inQuiry is a new form of inquiry into our own cultural identities that will improve our inner, thereby team agility ability™ to effectively communicate and deeply connect with others.

Part Three goes beyond Inner and Team Agility to share more about insights, research and practical case studies for those readers that are ready for the roadmap to Organisational Agility.

PART THREE

ORGANISATIONAL AGILITY ABILITY™

CHAPTER TWENTY
GOING BEYOND CULTURAL TRANSFORMATION

The purpose of this book is about how to reset your organisational culture by co-creating **culture-based performance.**

The journey started at the beginning of the book, in Part One, when we shared the value of understanding your individual human experience for your personal **inner agility ability™.**

Then we expanded the focus, in Part Two, on understanding that we all have separate realities. The important consideration is that our current state of mind is always changing moment to moment. These concepts are the foundations of co-creating high performance **team agility ability™.**

We have also shared how integrating Cultural inQuiry™ into your organisation will help implement your plans to support overall **organisational agility ability**™ and will continue in more detail in this Part Three.

The next step is to help you get started and to 'CQify' ® yourself, your team, and your organisation.

The following section outline the roadmap to start implementing a shift in your culture.

It is time to start....

First, let's...

Recap what Cultural inQuiry™ is

Cultural inQuiry™ is an opportunity to see the world with a fresh perspective. A chance to discover how cultural conditioning shapes our beliefs at an **individual** level.

Cultural inQuiry improves a **team** by encouraging us to see beyond the cultural conditioning that limits our capacity to connect, communicate, and collaborate with others. It helps improve recruitment and team morale, while also ensuring successful retention of valuable team members. Cultural inQuiry creates meaningful solution based team engagement.

Cultural inQuiry improves an **organisation** by developing and advancing a sustainable capability to co-create original and agile thinking. It creates opportunities for fresh insights to overcome challenges.

This is a game changing form of inquiry that places our identities in the centre of the human-to-human interaction. Once we understand how our human experience is created, our own inner agility ability to communicate and connect with others improves. It then expands into how to co-create the team's agility for culture-based performance.

Cultural inQuiry introduces a new paradigm for co-creating collective power towards next level organisational success.

Why Cultural inQuiry™ is pertinent to business performance

Cultural inQuiry™ provides the pathway to progressive human-to-human interactions, nurturing a psychologically agile and safe work environment to achieve inner, team and organisational agility. Research findings[5] attest to how Cultural inQuiry is improving interactions that can spiral into team synergy, breaking through people's limiting beliefs, stereotypes, and judgements.

Shifting from hierarchy to harmony by embedding Cultural inQuiry into the organisation will help maintain and develop a trust-based learning environment. When there is an open space to show up, individual creativity is unleashed to provide the organisational agility required to stay competitive. When leaders upskill their conventional leadership to become co-creators it is possible to create a team that flows with ongoing change. It is now time to challenge the status quo.

Cultural inQuiry is shifting focus from leadership towards co-creation. Individuals who bring a broad understanding and acceptance of diverse cultures to their professional endeavours are most likely to succeed in a global marketplace. This is due to multiculturalism and globalisation.

Multiculturalism refers to the co-existence of diverse cultures, each with its own physical space, language, and values.

Globalisation has now progressed into glocalisation, due to advancing technology and migration as a new norm, where people move from the country they were born. Glocalisation refers to the current state in which nations are interconnected by multiple economic, social, and political conduits, leading to interdependence among nations. The world population has shifted, it is no longer possible to categorise people from where they were born, as in most cases, parents and grandparents have migrated from another country. There are so many different cultural identities within each of us, which now advances the concept of multiculturalism.

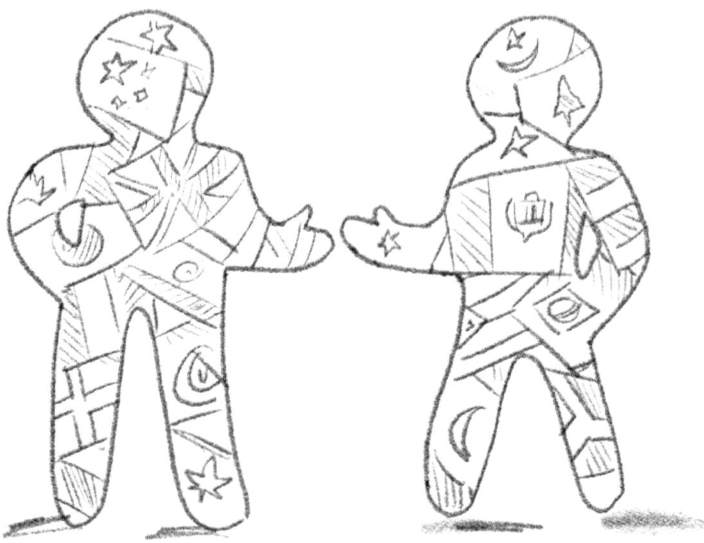

How would you, your organisation and the world change if we all replaced judgement with humility and curiosity?

Dr. Cari

Cultural inQuiry is an insight led journey that overcomes the majority of barriers to implementing organisational plans. Cultural inQuiry is the next level of human understanding, interaction, and organisation culture change management. It is not a training session, it is not a transformation initiative, it is not a mindset, it is not another leadership approach, it is the new way of consciously being, co-creating, communicating, connecting, and contributing to a healthy organisational and personal life.

Cultural inQuiry™ is the foundation for culture-based performance.

For a better work culture, people need to be free from borders and departmental silos and to relinquish the use of stereotypes and labels that define others. In this way we can appreciate our uniqueness as glocal citizens, while consciously participating in both personal and business development.

Every type of organisational challenge can be reframed from a human solution perspective using Cultural inQuiry. This enables a reduction in resistance, discomfort, discontent, and suffering to move towards a process of healing. Once we understand ourselves, meaning our own schema, and keep reflecting and acknowledging how our cultural identities are creating our world view, we can trust the process, build strong connections, and thrive amidst VUCA, BANI or whatever acronym is next.

Creating and maintaining a psychologically safe foundation for human-to-human connection and performance, combined with having a responsive versus reactive state of mind, and integrating Cultural inQuiry with co-creation principles at the core of your operation benefits all participants and establishes an organisational agility that stands the ever increasingly complex world we live in.

Dr. Jacqui

Organisational Agility Ability

Creativity is a key to innovation.
Innovation is a key to agility.
Agility is a key to next level performance....
So, the time is now to co-create your Organisational Agility Ability™.

The Agility Ability

Overall ***Agility Ability***™ is when the organisational culture is based on a foundation of our individual inner agility. This includes achieving a psychological agile and safe space that supports a responsive ethos where individual creativity fuels innovation. When individual team members are in a responsive state, it elevates collaboration success with agility ability.

The momentum of the team's collective effort can be achieved with only a few people in this responsive state at a time, so not everyone needs to have these states for the team to thrive. When there are clusters of teams in flow throughout the whole organisation, it is possible to experience a new level of performance that only this level of agility ability can accomplish.

The individual characteristics of Agility Ability™

The individual characteristics of agility ability™ come in many forms. This includes any number of the following that, individually or combined, support the development of our agility ability from an individual (inner), team and organisational perspective:

Curious
Seek surprises
Attracted to adventure
Supportive
Edgewalkers
Co-creators
Reflective
Non-judgmental

BOLDLY self-aware
Dream TEAM
Love a data deep dive
Responsive
SEE the UNSEEN
Clarity
Risk thrivers
Kind to self and others

Open minded
Critical Friend®
Challenges bias, judgments and status quo
Relentlessly
Go beyond brainstorming to freedom in flow –
Compassionate

Connectedness
Life-long passionate learners
Understand separate realities
Embrace the power of SPACE
Globally positioned (experienced)
Explorers
Creative
Collaborative

Each characteristic has been touched on within this book. Some, in greater detail than others. All work as aspects of the agility ability journey in delivery a roadmap from inner, to team, to organisational agility ability.

SEE the UNSEEN
open
minded
Clarity
Glocally positioned (experienced)
risk thrivers
Dream TEAM
attracted to adventure
Co-creators
Understand Separate Realities
Responsive
Go Beyond Brainstorming to Freedom in Flow – connectedness
Embrace the Power of SPACE
Edgewalkers
seek surprises
curious
life-long passionate learners
Explorers
BOLDLY self-aware
love a data deep dive
Critical Friend
Challenge Bias and Judgments and Status Quo relentlessly

CHAPTER TWENTY-ONE
ROADMAP FOR AGILITY ABILITY™

The roadmap to Culture-Based Performance™

Our roadmap to Culture-Based Performance moves from curiosity, through a series of phases, to organisational agility ability™ and staying in the flow thereafter once established.

Let's move through the phases one by one....

PHASE ONE - be COURAGEOUSLY CURIOUS about yourself and others

First, we encourage an honest exploration about what makes you **YOU**. What we have shared is that over 85% of research participants[5] did not even know they had unconscious bias or understand how this influenced their day-to-day perception of the world. If we are not aware of the information, we are selecting that is fuelling our decision making, it is not possible to accept others until we understand ourselves. Our unconscious bias drives our automatic pilot. Awareness and acknowledgement disrupt our automatic pilot and help us to be more open and accepting of ourselves and others.

If you have time, consider the following exercise, and the ones that follow to embed your thinking and aid learning and development of your own insights. As previous, these are optional but designed to maximise the benefit of reading this book.

CQ Exercise:

We invite you to begin with some reflective questioning. This should be done in a calm and responsive state of mind, so find a quiet place or somewhere you are at your most relaxed to begin thinking about the following questions:

What do you believe about the world and WHY?

Then start by taking time to reflect on why you do things a certain way?

It is important to always be kind and gentle with ourselves throughout this process and resist the temptation to judge or criticise ourselves. What our research confirms is that you are only one thought away about changing any belief that is no longer true or working for you now.

CQ If you can make time or when you have about 15 minutes, we located a link that has a very powerful test developed by Harvard that shows how our unconscious bias impacts our judgements, stereotypes and decision making. We encourage you to check it out if you can. There are a number of categories to choose from and explore. At the end, the results give you more information on what type of biases are at play in your world. It is very interesting and worth taking the time to check out even one category to start with. We are always surprised by the outcomes, have fun, be curious and go to: https://implicit.harvard.edu/implicit/selectatouchtestv2.html

PHASE TWO - Move from REACTIVE to RESPONSIVE

We would like to suggest that you begin taking time to observe and acknowledge what your emotional triggers are. Learning that it is our thinking that is creating our feelings in the moment that completely changed our own life experiences. When we can self soothe by knowing how to disrupt an ego flare up with ways that can calm our mind down.

Just as a reminder, it is when we are conscious in the moment, we can shift from being reactive to being responsive. Responsive teams leverage the most creativity and successful collaboration. So, keep observing your own mind to acknowledge when your balloon head is inflating, while observing what level you are at in the state of mind elevator will be helpful to navigate towards a responsive state. Then if your elevator is in the basement, you can be gentle with yourself and stay away from big life decisions until you are lifted back up to or above the main level. When we can learn what helps each of us personally to return to a calm state, it becomes possible to show up differently in all aspects of our life.

PHASE THREE - INSIGHT-LED COMMUNICATION and EMERGENT ACTIONS

Insight-led communication and the resultant emergent actions are the core of creativity, the heart of innovation. It only takes one current to start the wave of change.

Even if only one person on the team is clear and present it can positively impact the whole team. If the majority of the team is in a responsive state, they can allow new thinking and fresh perspectives to evolve. Our ideas are inspired from within, just like the name **In**sights. Actions emerge from these new thoughts and ideas so that our plans can be implemented.

This phase can sometimes be the most challenging, as our cultural conditioning can overshadow the power of how insights can surprise us all. Most of us still believe we need to show up with lists, meeting plans, and allocated time slots to be productive.

We are suggesting you let some of that go to make space to try a new style of meeting. Don't panic, there are times when we do need to revert back to a list of items and time allocation, there is still a place for these planning style meetings. As long as there is more insight led meetings, co-creators have the agility ability to flow over any daily distraction and stay focused on the overall plan. We never know what new thinking or ideas will emerge out of a conversation or meeting when the right formula is in place to inspire insight-led communication.

It is impossible for us to share the details of what you will discover when you engage in this phase, as the experience will be unique to you and your team. The exciting part is when there is a collective team desire to let go of strict meeting agendas with planned outcomes, the freedom for new ideas to flow is what fuels creativity and innovation.

PHASE FOUR - ENGAGE YOUR CRITICAL FRIEND®

There is something so helpful about having a **critical friend®** to bounce your ideas off, letting them challenge your thinking to inspire you to consider different perspectives for robust decision making that has no hidden agendas and reduced biases. There is a deep level of trust and psychological safety required to openly engage with confronting our insecurities, sharing fears, and pushing our egos aside for an authentic connection with others.

We can share that our team is always engaging our critical friends because this produces the best outcomes. We also actively focus on how to co-create any vision or goal we are working towards. Critical friends push us beyond what we ever thought possible and provide the deepest personal growth opportunities that contribute to our overall performance in both our private and business lives.

PHASE FIVE - IMPLEMENT and REFLECT

This phase is just like it says on the Tin! Implement the plans and keep reflecting on your implementation to check that all is as it should be. This is an ongoing process based on a cycle of action, as shown below, make progress - reflect - make more progress - reflect. Even if progress means discovering barriers, the space for reflection disrupts them. The reflection part is critical so everyone on the team can flag up potential barriers and overcome any other obstacles before they fester into something bigger.

The implementation phase is linked to all the other phases. By using our **LENS Framework**™ as guidance, it is possible to anchor all efforts here to measure alignment and desired outcomes.

This focus and agility ability™ will keep you and your team on track with minimal detours. When everyone is progressing, reflecting, and moving forward it is possible to experience how this impacts outcomes. The ability to navigate all types of uncertainty can dissolve these barriers that previously grinded a halt to your plans. Instead, you and the team are moving into flow.

PHASE SIX - STAY in FLOW

Flow can navigate and overcome barriers such as our social mask, ego and fear that keep us stuck in a toxic workplace culture. Shifting from hierarchy to harmony by turning **ME** to **WE** are the beginning of becoming co-creators. When we can all be accountable and work together it is possible to co-creating high performing collaborative teams.

Then you begin to see how this shift helps everyone to remain focused and implement plans, regardless of the distraction. This level of resilience and perseverance is based on being responsive, by recognising when our balloon heads are inflating and reminding ourselves that we all are experiencing separate realities, we can stay in flow. Co-creators thrive by integrating Cultural inQuiry into their daily practice and team so they can actively achieve **culture-based performance.**

Take your organisation's agility ability to the next level by changing the focus from:

Leadership to CO-CREATION.

Mindset to STATE OF MIND.

Trust to ACCOUNTABILITY.

Communication to CONNECTION.

Being Stuck to Organisational FLOW...

Each component has a distinct human and human-to-human focus.

By bringing together the varied expertise of individuals through co-creation, the end combined efforts outperform us as individuals alone. This moves us from individuals, to teams, and onto an organisational agility focus in achieving greater culture-based performance.

- Dr. Jacqui

CHAPTER TWENTY-TWO
THE CQify LENS FRAMEWORK™ - a focus on people

The **CQify LENS Framework**™ is focused on the human element to deliver an organisation's strategy plan and improve performance by leveraging the organisational culture. Each of the four aspects combine to provide greater likelihood of implementing your strategy plan.

Leveraging Culture to

Explore and acknowledge our own individual schema. This understanding needs to include how everyone has different cultural conditioning that is influencing their own view of the world.

In using Cultural inQuiry to understand ourselves on a continual learning journey by being curious, we can contribute to co-created intentions.

Leveraging culture is connecting people who:

- Embrace curiosity about themselves and others,
- Care with intention and purpose, and
- Thrive on continuous learning.

Encourage

A place that is created within the team and organisation that is considered to be psychologically safe to show up as our authentic selves. Understanding that both are required, we need to encourage ourselves and others to focus on personal **and** professional growth and development.

Cultural inQuiry integrates the understanding of how to co-create these spaces and learning opportunities.

Encourage is making space to:

- Nurturing a psychologically safe place to connect,
- Focus on personal and professional growth and development.

Non-judgemental Insights

Is where the unexpected inspiration and ideas come from the team. Insights are personal ideas that have no specific formula and are generated where your mind has unlimited access to all possibilities and not confined by expectation.

Cultural inQuiry is designed specifically to focus on how to generate non-judgmental insights, just like a surfer waiting in the ocean for that perfect wave to ride.

Non-judgemental insights come from:

- Being responsive and generating creative ideas through a collective team effort towards a vision,
- Fostering collaboration within an inclusive team environment.

Strategy Implementation

Is putting those plans into action and overcoming the day-to-day distractions.

Our insight-led action inquiry cycles unleash the co-creation of high performing teams. This is when collaboration peaks with a full view of the organisation's co-created culture-based performance.

Strategy implementation acts as a catalyst so that:

- Regardless of any barriers there is a relentless team flow that is resilient, adaptable, and sustainable.

CHAPTER TWENTY-THREE
Cultural inQuiry Cycles©

At CQify, we offer the benefit of using our team to co-create a Culture-Based Performance™ with your team using our Culture InQuiry Cycles© for your AGILITY ABILITY™....

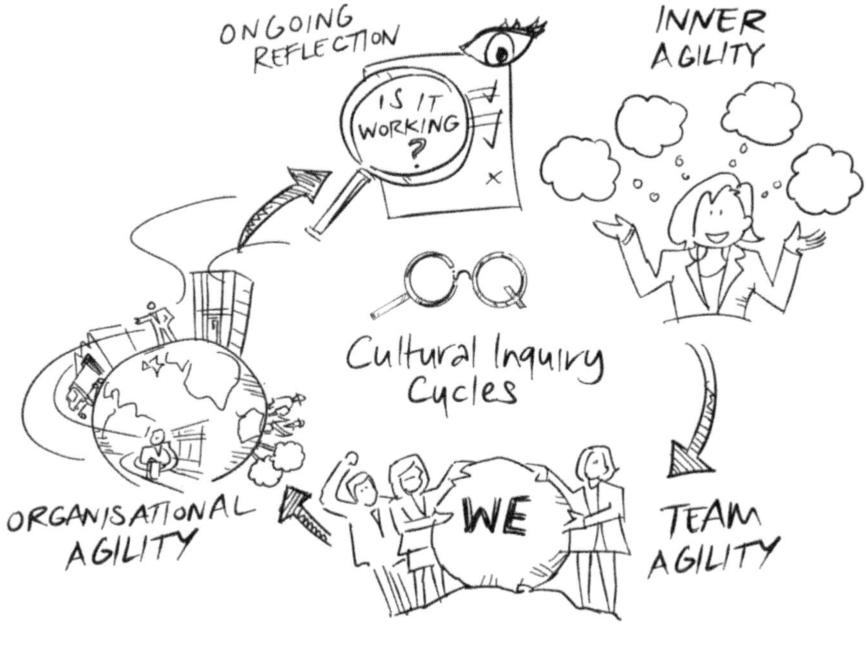

Cultural Inquiry Cycles

When you begin using Cultural inQuiry Action Cycles© here is what can happen....

For your ...

Inner Agility

YOU will learn how to:

- Become an effective co-creator,
- Acknowledge the impact of cultural conditioning in day-to-day life,
- Become more responsive and less reactive,
- Integrate the concept of separate realities directly into your life,
- Successfully ride the state of mind elevator,
- Calm the mind to experience our resilience,
- Create a psychologically agile inner space for insights to happen.

Using Cultural inQuiry™ for...

Team Agility

The TEAM will learn how to:

- Overcome misunderstandings and ego flare ups,
- Connect meaningfully with everyone's separate realities,
- Acknowledge everyone's state of mind elevator,
- Create a psychologically safe and agile team space for insights to happen,
- Learn effective strategies to work as a **creative** team,
- Explore possibilities for better **collaboration** with others,
- **Co-create** a powerful team culture that is genuinely **inclusive.**

Using Cultural inQuiry™ for...

Organisational Agility

The ORGANISATION will discover:

- When one team works at this level, change will occur organically,
- When some teams operate at this level significant change happens,
- When many teams work at this level culture-based performance flourishes.

and to stay in the flow with...

Ongoing Reflection .....

- Co-create reflection with your critical friends®....

To find out more you are invited to get in touch and book a complimentary discovery call.

Scan the QR code below to connect to our website for contact details.

CQify
Culture-based
Performance

Alternatively go to www.cqify.com or email us at info@cqify.com

CHAPTER TWENTY-FOUR
ORGANISATIONAL AGILITY ABILITY™ MANIFESTO

To CEOs, Leadership Teams, Entrepreneurs, Teachers and Learners and everyone interested in shifting towards: **CO-CREATION**

- Be **responsive** - jolt out of automatic pilot, stop self-medicating, self-sabotaging and seek calm.
- Use inner inquiry to give you fresh insight to **LEAP** over the barriers in your life and work.
- Passionately **UNLEARN** to **LEARN** about everything.
- **Curiosity** is the key to living fearlessly conscious in the moment.
- Our **individual culture** is always developing with every new experience, everyone is original.
- Embracing our **Glocal citizenship** - we are all made up from many different cultures.
- **Recognising** when we are having an **ego flare up** and knowing how to return to a state of calm.
- Be **open hearted**, to connect with others deeply, we understand everyone has a separate reality.

- When smothering occurs through ego-led leadership, micromanagement, manipulation, hidden agendas, fear, overwhelm and conflict - our **reactive** mode is triggered, and creativity is lost.
- Our **purpose** is clear when there is an ethical cause and contribution, where insights flourish.
- Believe in **accountability** and always doing what you say you will do or share what happened.
- Always **unconditionally acknowledge** the conditions we put on ourselves and others.
- There is no need for any type of **transformation**, we are perfect as we are when we are open to fresh thinking and perspectives.
- When we are all in **FLOW**, collaboration, connection, and co-creation unleashes....
- **Together** we can achieve the next level of individual, team, and organisational **agility ability**!™

Higher quality is achievable through co-creating than through individual efforts alone.
That is...by bringing together the varied expertise of individuals through co-creation, the end combined efforts outperform us as individuals alone.

- Dr. Jacqui

This moves us from inner agility, to team agility, and onto organisational agility ability™.

CQ KEY INSIGHTS OF PART THREE

In summary, the key insights, or takeaways from Part Three include:

- **Cultural inQuiry:**
    - Is an opportunity to see the world with a **fresh perspective** and discover how cultural conditions shape our beliefs at an individual level.
    - Creates meaningful solution based **team** engagement.
    - Improves an **organisation** by developing and advancing a sustainable capability to co-create original and agile thinking.
    - Creates opportunities for fresh insights to overcome challenges.
    - Provides the pathway to progressive human-to-human interactions, nurturing a psychologically agile work environment to achieve **inner, team and organisational agility.**
    - Is an insight led journey that overcomes the majority of barriers to implementing organisational plans.
    - ***Is the foundation for culture-based performance.***
- Globalisation has now progressed into **glocalisation,** due to advancing technology and migration as a new norm.
- Once we understand how our human experience is created, our own **inner agility ability**™ to communicate and connect with others will improve.
- Overall ***Agility Ability***™ is when the organisational culture is based on a foundation of our individual inner agility.
- **Cultural-Based Performance** moves from curiosity, through a series of phases, to **organisational agility ability**™ and staying in the flow thereafter once established. To get there:
    - Be courageously curious.
    - Move from reactive to responsive.

  - Insight-led communication and emergent actions are the core of creativity, the heart of innovation.
  - Engage your critical friend® to bounce ideas off.
  - Implement and reflect.
  - Stay in the flow to navigate and overcome barriers.
- **CQify LENS Framework**™ is focused on the human element to deliver an organisation's strategy plan and improve performance by leveraging the organisational culture.
  - **Leveraging culture to** explore and acknowledge our own schema.
  - **Encourage** a place to show our authentic selves.
  - **Non-judgemental insights** through unexpected inspiration and ideas from the team.
  - **Strategy implementation** in putting plans into action and overcoming distractions.
- **Cultural inQuiry Cycles**© enable co-creation of a performance-based culture for **agility ability**™**.**
- Take your **organisations agility ability**™ to the next level by changing focus from:
  - Leadership to CO-CREATION.
  - Mindset to STATE OF MIND.
  - Trust to ACCOUNTABILITY.
  - Communication to CONNECTION.
  - Being Stuck to Organisational FLOW...

If you would like to speak to someone about co-creating a performance based culture or any other bespoke engagement for you, your team or organisation, scan the QR code below to connect to our website for contact details.

CQify
Culture-based **Performance**

Alternatively go to www.cqify.com or email us at info@cqify.com

If you would like to have your ideas challenged or bounce around some ideas on a decision you need to make, we are here to help. Just simply scan the QR code below to contact a **critical friend**®.

Critical **Friend**

PART FOUR

CASE STUDIES

CASE STUDY ONE - Glocalisation

Dr. Kennedy, who wrote our forward, conducted Glocalisation[1] research at a large multinational company to explore challenges being faced by the organisation developing culturally and linguistically appropriate web marketing content for its customers around the globe. He investigated conflicting perspectives around culture, linguistic and governance issues amongst those arguing for global one-size-fits-all perspectives to achieve cost efficiency and brand consistency, and those arguing for local perspectives that would deliver tailored web content for each market which could resonate with local customers and drive business locally. Web marketing content developed for use around the world, was frequently found not to be suitable for adaptation or direct use by the regional product marketing teams. Using Hollensen's's[9] glocalisation framework as an analytical tool, Dr. Kennedy found that progress could be made addressing the conflicting perspectives across the organisation around cultural, linguistic and governance issues by searching for the presence of glocal dynamics.

Dr. Kennedy looked for and found 'glocal' dynamics that could support achieving balance and harmony between the conflicting global and local perspectives.

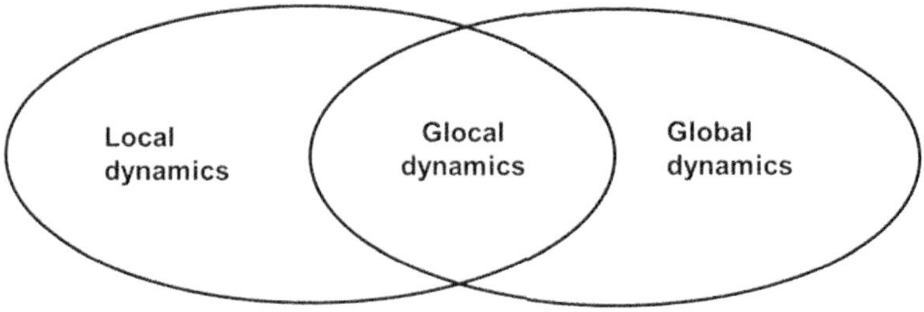

This required an understanding of the human-to-human interaction as outlined in this book that is based on Dr. Cari's foundational research[5] and built on over the past three years.

Dr. Kennedy exploration of glocal dynamics led to a review of existing hub and spoke organisational approaches. This involved many of the concepts used in infrastructure configurations[6] studied by Dr. Jacqui in her research. Adopting glocalisation approaches suggested moving from a centralised hub and spoke organisational structure towards a blend of a centralised and de-centralised multi-hub organisational structure.

Of interest, Dr. Kennedy found what originally was considered a problem concerning cultural and linguistic issues ended up being conflicting perspectives on these and governance issues. As suggested by Dr. Cari's research, human-to-human interactions were key to understanding the problem. When conflicting perspectives concerning linguistic, cultural, and governance issues were studied, addressed and communication improved, both the local and global perspectives could be accommodated by adopting a glocal approach.

CASE STUDY TWO - Customer centric expectations against the actual experience

Dr. Jacqui undertook a consultancy where the organisation was failing to meet customer expectations with an ever-increasing rate of customer complaints about poor services, non-delivery, and delays in responses. The organisation had engaged a consultant to develop a renewed vision and mission, and five-year strategy twelve months before. Nothing had changed since, there was no engagement with the staff in delivering against the vision, mission, or strategy. Sales were dropping, services ad hoc, and morale down. There was a clear communication gap.

In the first week, through one-on-one interviews, small group discussions and gleaning information prior to setting up a survey across the staff and considering how to best engage with customers to seek their thoughts, some interesting 'invisible' issues came to light. Staff were engaged with to help review the previous vision and mission statements yet had only seen the final version on the website. Neither were communicated nor posted anywhere across the organisation. There were no values listing visible either. The strategy plan was compiled through a management workshop and follow-up discussions, staff claim to having never seen the strategy nor the content. Yet they were expected to deliver against the plan approved by the board. There were gaps emerging in the communication channels.

With no clear plan evident, staff were so focused on the business as usual, or what they thought was business as usual, they were on a continual cycle of automatic pilot and missed opportunities to not only develop themselves but advance the organisation towards the 'agreed' vision. They were blind to what was happening around them, cocooning themselves in creating no time for any reflection or insights to emerge, and losing customers in the process. The lack of knowledge of the strategy, targets and direction was impacting their thinking and focus.

Complaints were responded with reference to being too busy, it was someone else's problem or issue, and customers were being too demanding. No one took the time to review the complaints or follow up with the customers. Looking at the records, many issues could have been addressed quite quickly and increased customer satisfaction, and the bottom line at the same time. Individually, each staff member believed they were being a team player and customer-centric in their focus. The customer complaints indicated otherwise.

Through a series of discussions and workshops, staff and customer survey, plans became clearer, greater awareness of the misunderstandings, lack of communication and assumptions being made evolved. Customers indicated that they now felt heard, and actions were being taken. Complaints started to drop off. Staff indicated greater awareness of expectations from both the organisation and customers, where the organisation was heading and how they fitted into that direction.

Staff and management, and the leaders were talking. Leaders came out of their offices and actively communicated with staff, reducing the 'them and us' view and improving understanding of what was happening across the organisation. The insights aided further planning and direction setting in a more co-creational approach that was communicated across the organisation. Working with the leaders generated ways to embed the changes and reduce returning to old practices that did not serve them, the staff, customers, or shareholders. The reactive mode was moving towards greater responsiveness.

It wasn't until a reflective mirror exercise was put up to the staff members that greater understanding that their self-sabotaging was happening to the level of challenging their ongoing roles. It became their respective 'ah ha' moment, their understanding of how their reaction mode was creating the challenges they faced. Over subsequent weeks, many, not all, changed differing aspects of their approach, resulting in a reduction in customer complaints and enquiries for development / training or involvement in exercises / projects coming up.

A similar exercise with leaders generated greater insights into why what they thought should happen wasn't, what level of communication and key messages were going out or not going out, and what options were available to them to address the challenges they now faced. Greater awareness of the misunderstandings around the process twelve months prior offered the opportunity to start addressing those misunderstandings and increase active engagement with staff.

CASE STUDY THREE - Toxic work culture

A group of company directors that we know are interested in selling their company. The organisation is in a niche market, is viable and generating a profit. Although there have been a few key investors looking to buy this company, it has never sold.

On the surface, the company is viable, but the toxic workplace culture is blocking a sale. During the due diligence process when potential purchasers start analysing the company processes and people, it is impossible to hide a toxic work culture that emanates throughout the organisation. Key people are leaving, head-hunted by the competition and there is an overall disengagement of team members.

Digging deeper, the potential reason from our perspective is simple, there are no collective leadership initiatives being rolled out due to the lack of respect between the directors. This evident lack of respect is resulting in a high level of incompetencies and toxicities throughout the whole organisation that is picked up during the due diligence process. The organisation's reputation is being tarnished by negative staff experiences combined with the ongoing lack of interest in sale.

The fear that the organisation could collapse is driving staff to find alternate employment. This lack of transparent communication from the leadership team is compounding the issue with fewer people to undertake the duties needed. Whenever a key person leaves, they are also taking their network and loyal customer base with them. Customers are becoming disgruntled and moving to the competition, further compounding the issue.

The blind spot is that each director believes it's the other one's fault, and blame will not change any outcomes. Each display an ego-led style in their leadership along with the misuse of power is contributing to the toxicity that exists within the organisation. They are each acting as a blocker to the sale through their actions that demonstrate their perceived power, level of self-importance and letting their ego drive their decision making.

When there is solely an ego-led style of leadership, some of the common symptoms exhibited are that they are never wrong, apathy towards key people quitting, board room bullying, and no desire for personal or professional development. These symptoms are evident in this organisation. Unless they are addressed, there is a potential for the organisation to not sell and eventually close, leaving the directors worse off than if they addressed the current situation together.

From our observations, there is a blind belief that they are the best and who cares about the rest or each other. It has created a no-win situation that needs to be addressed for the organisation to survive.

CASE STUDY FOUR - Individual culture triggering barriers to communication

Dr. Cari undertook research in an organisation where language, trust and internal conflict were blocking the collaboration between the differing members in a European based network[5]. This was preventing the implementation of strategies focused on improving skills to nurture diverse relationships. From a basis of learning at an individual level, Dr. Cari encouraged the recognition and acknowledgement of their own biases, judgements and stereotypes being influenced by the central role of culture, impacting communication. Awareness of this 'schema' became the starting point of their journey towards achieving collaboration.

The network members were taken through how the role of culture posed challenges simply with the different interpretations of shared terms and actions. Through this research process a key outcome was the realisation about how these misunderstandings impact communication effectiveness between people from different cultures. Improving the understanding of how our individual schema is vulnerable to our cultural conditioning introduced new perspectives. This included exploring perceptions of the benefits of the network, around barriers to communication, building multicultural relationships versus same culture relationships, cultural stereotypes, engagement and growth perceptions.

Challenges of remote working locations, diversity, and collaboration knowledge required the realignment of strategies by centralising culture at the heart of the member analysis, communications, team building and overall leadership capabilities. As a result, the cultural impact on personal biases, stereotypes, and judgments and how that contributed to barriers of diverse communication became clearer. Strategies were devised to reduce barriers of language, gain a consensus about the definition of trust, reducing misunderstandings and how our unacknowledged schema could be disrupting multicultural communication.

Working with the network members to shift their perspective through critical reflection on the role of culture within their schema aided the awareness of their personal views of reality. Members were encouraged to mindfully share or acknowledge personal cultural stereotypes, which exposed them to being vulnerable in the diverse global group. This process of acknowledgment was uncomfortable and posed an emotional risk to experience change with individual beliefs, biases, or stereotypes. A couple of different members did not put themselves forward for leadership or speaking roles due to their belief that their national culture was not generally respected enough. This shows the power culture has on stereotypes and individual perception.

Members were at differing stages of awareness, from unaware different cultures existed, to avoiding diverse situations, to heightened awareness. This variability was addressed through disclosure of personal information around cultural norms, increasing trust and insights to increase awareness across the members. Fear from a lack of understanding of another's culture generated avoidance behaviour in some, where they avoided participation through fear of offending or acceptance by other members, that needed to be addressed to improve the overall functioning of the network.

In exploring individual knowledge or awareness of their own schema, the influence of culture was able to be interpreted by asking questions such as:

1. What are the member's perceptions of the benefits of the network?
2. How do the members perceive barriers of communication?
3. How does the member's individual schema help / hinder with multicultural relationships versus same culture relationships?
4. How do the member's cultural stereotypes influence communication?
5. What are the member's perceptions of engagement and growth opportunities within the organisation?

Dr. Cari's research saw the shifting of members actions towards adapting within the diverse environment. The importance of individual acknowledgment of how culture influences their schema before diverse communication can be improved for collaboration to occur was identified. Existing beliefs were able to be changed in a trusting environment to generate sustainable change. A focus on individual unique schema overcame the complexities of the members' multiple cultural identities. This realised greater collaboration. By placing the impact of culture at the heart of inquiry, combined with a collective leadership approach, the change was able to be embedded and sustained.

Dr. Cari found that our cultural conditioning does impact individual members' perceptions of reality. This understanding indicated that for change to be more effective it needed to be addressed at an individual level first by confronting the barriers of diverse communication. Barriers such as language, lack of trust, conflict and unacknowledged schemas disrupt multicultural communication. These needed to be addressed by shifting perspectives with critical self-reflection, including acknowledging the role of culture within the schema that generates our personal views of reality.

What became clear was that when stakeholders are accountable for their own perceptions and aware that their schemas can change, it is possible to confront the barriers of diverse communication. Awareness of culture, combined with a willingness to learn about different cultures, was a good start to develop the members' cultural intelligence. The learning changed the perceptions and member behaviours, improving engagement and collaboration within the network.

This collaboration created a synergy and bond between the members. Failure to work through this process and collectively contribute to member perspectives could have resulted in continued conflict and lack of engagement.

To establish this delicate process of balance, it needed to be acknowledged that this could turn into conflict if not conducted mindfully. During the moments of vulnerability, it was necessary to be cautious in how context was provided so feelings were acknowledged to guide participants through the discomfort without causing conflict. It was not possible to stimulate such a deep level of discussion without trust. Dr. Cari observed that all participants began to acknowledge their schema while identifying the sources of their beliefs, which were founded from the culture they were raised in.

This journey of joint discovery of schemas was simultaneously supported with ongoing critical reflection to bring unconscious decisions to the conscious mind. This confirmed that living and working in different cultures also impact our individual schemas with multiple cultural identities. Regardless of how many cultures the members exposed themselves to, it did not equate to possessing cultural intelligence. Therefore, it was necessary to begin at the individual level to understand how their own multiple cultural identities influenced their reality and ability for collective impact.

Furthermore, Dr. Cari validated how mindful awareness of the role of culture penetrates the individual schema and influences participants' perceptions of reality. By gently challenging individual perceptions, it was possible to change original beliefs, biases, and stereotypes to overcome barriers of language, trust, and conflict.

Impact on leaders to consider

In a leadership role, it is necessary to share a trusting relationship to reveal the raw truth of each person's perceptions. Without going through this process with critical self-reflection guided by a trustful leader who will not pass judgment, it could be a challenge to learn about how we all think differently based on personal experiences. When a leader places the role of culture at the heart of inquiry, it is possible to expose stakeholders to other perspectives through understanding their own limitations.

Diverse communication is complex and without navigating through the swampy land of self-discovery it could contribute to further barriers of communication. Culture can potentially be related to as the compass that guides our core values and beliefs. Neglecting the impact of culture may continue to block trust, causing conflict, resulting with lack of collaboration across diverse teams.

PART FIVE

REFERENCES

REFERENCES

1. Kennedy, D. (2021) 'Investigating conflicting perspectives at a software multinational concerning its efforts to produce culturally and linguistically appropriate web content for its customers around the globe', *UK: The University of Liverpool.*
2. Marr, B. (2012) *Key Performance Indicators (KPI): The 75 measures every manager needs to know*. UK: Pearson.
3. Niven, P.R. and Lamorte, B. (2016) *Objectives and key results: Driving focus, alignment, and engagement with OKRs*. UK: John Wiley & Sons.
4. Kaplan. R. S. and Norton, D. P. (1992) 'The Balanced Scorecard: Measures that drive performance', *Harvard Business Review,* January-February 1992, pp. 71-79.
5. Leyshon, C. L. (2020) 'How does an individual's culture trigger barriers of communication in a diverse environment? The case of a European Enforcement Network', *UK: The University of Liverpool.*
6. Hiddlestone-Mumford, J. (2019) 'Transitioning from a traditional office to an activity-based work environment', *UK: University of Liverpool.*

7. Amoo, N., Hiddlestone-Mumford, J., Ruzibuka, J. and Akwei, C. (2019) 'Conceptualizing and Measuring Strategy Implementation – a multi-dimensional view', *Strategic Change,* 28(6), pp. 445-4677.
8. Amoo, N. and Hiddlestone-Mumford, J. (2017) 'Development and Validation of Multi-Dimensional Measures for Strategy Implementation', *Strategy & Organizational Behaviour eJournal,* 6(22). *SSRN: 3008597*
9. Hollenson, S. (2014) *Global Marketing.* 6th edn. Harlow: Pearson Education.
10. Hiddlestone-Mumford, J. (2021) 'Adapting the workplace for disability inclusion and generational change', *Doctoral Conference in Strategy, Corporate Governance, Innovation and International Business,* De Montfort University, Leicester, UK.
11. Hiddlestone-Mumford, J. (2022) 'Changing the workplace environment to enhance disability inclusion', *British Academy of Management Conference,* University of Manchester Alliance Manchester Management School, UK.
12. Hiddlestone-Mumford, J. (2020) 'Strategic use of Practice-of-inquiry to Change Workplace Environments', *Journal of Organizational Psychology,* 20(1) ISSN: 2158-3609.
13. Quinn, L. and Dalton, M. (2009) 'Leading for sustainability: implementing the tasks of leadership', *Corporate Governance: The International Journal of Business in Society,* *9*(1), pp. 21-38.
14. Kaleem, Y., Asad, S. and Khan, H. (2016) 'Leadership styles & using appropriate styles in different circumstances', *Sir Syed University of Engineering and Technology, Karachi-Pakistan.*

15. Oberer, B. and Erkollar, A. (2018) 'Leadership 4.0: Digital leaders in the age of industry 4.0.', *InternationalJjournal of Organizational Leadership*, pp. 1-9.
16. Formica, S. and Sfodera, F. (2022) 'The Great Resignation and Quiet Quitting paradigm shifts: An overview of current situation and future research directions', *Journal of Hospitality Marketing & Management,* 31(8), pp. 899-907.
17. Ruhle, S. A., Breitsohl, H., Aboagye, E., Baba, V., Biron, C., Correia Leal, C., Dietz, C., Ferreira, A.I., Gerich, J., Johns, G. and Karanika-Murray, M. (2020) '"To work, or not to work, that is the question"–Recent trends and avenues for research on presenteeism', *European Journal of Work and Organizational Psychology*, *29*(3), pp. 344-363.
18. OECD.stat (2023) 'Health Status: Absence from work due to illness', *Organisation for Economic Co-operation and Development*. Available at: https://stats.oecd.org/index.aspx?queryid=30123
19. Anderson, P. (1969) 'Components of the national culture', *New Left Review,* 1(50), pp. 214-284.
20. Brecheisen, J. (2023) 'Diversity and Inclusion. Research: Where employees think companies' DEIB efforts are failing', *Harvard Business Review,* March 09 2023. Available at: https://hbr.org/2023/03/research-where-employees-think-companies-deib-efforts-are-failing
21. Rosen, Y. (2014) 'Comparability of conflict opportunities in human-to-human and human-to-agent online collaborative problem solving', *Technology, Knowledge and Learning,* 18(3), pp. 1-27.

22. van den Hout, J.J.J. and Davis, O.C. (2022) 'Promoting the Emergence of Team Flow in Organizations', *International Journal of Applied Positive Psychology, 7,* pp. 143–189.
23. Hiddlestone-Mumford, J. (2021) 'Workplace environmental change to facilitate flexible practices in the face of Covid-19 fallout and how that has impacted the work environment itself', *British Academy of Management Conference*, Lancaster University Management School, UK.
24. Lynch, A. Q. (1985) 'The Myers-Briggs Type indicator: A tool for appreciating employee and client diversity', *Journal of Employment Counselling*, *22*(3), pp. 104-109.
25. Furlow, L. (2000) 'Job profiling: Building a winning team using behavioral assessments', *JONA: The Journal of Nursing Administration*, 30(3), pp. 107-111.
26. Li. S, Wang. Y, Xue. J, Zhao. N, Zhu. T. (2020) 'The impact of COVID-19 epidemic declaration on psychological consequences: A study on active Weibo users', *International Journal of Environmental Research and Public Health,*. 17(6), pp. 2032.
27. Ketprepakorn, N. and Kantabutra, S. (2022) 'Towards an organizational theory of sustainability culture', *Sustainable Production and Consumption*, 32, pp. 638-654.
28. United Nations (2023) *Global Issue: Migration,* Available at: https://www.un.org/en/global-issues/migration
29. Aghaei. S., Nematbakhsh, M. A. and Farsani, H. K. (2012) 'Evolution of the World Wide Web: From Web 1.0 to Web 4.0', *International Journal of Web & Semantic Technology* (IJWesT), 3(1), pp. 1-10.

30. ITU G5 Accelerator (2023) 'From traditional telecommunication environment to digital landscape', available at: https://gen5.digital/explainers/the-story-behind-five-generations-of-regulation-g1-to-g5/
31. Brecheisen, J. (2023) 'Research: Where employees think companies' DEIB efforts are failing', *Harvard Business Review*, March 2023, available at: https://hbr.org/2023/03/research-where-employees-think-companies-deib-efforts-are-failing
32. Serafeim, G. (2020) 'Social-impact efforts that create real value', *Harvard Business Review,* September-October 2020, pp. 1-20. available at: https://hbr.org/2014/01/what-vuca-really-means-for-you
33. Bennett, N. and Lemoine, G. J. (2014) 'What VUCA really means for you', *Harvard Business Review*, 92(1/2), available at: https://hbr.org/2014/01/what-vuca-really-means-for-you
34. de Godoy, M.F. and Ribas Filho, D. (2021) 'Facing the BANI world', *International Journal of Nutrology*, *14*(2), pp. 33-33.
35. Whittaker, M., Crawford, K., Dobbe, R., Fried, G., Kaziunas, E., Mathur, V., West, S. M., Richardson, R., Schultz, J. and Schwartz, O. (2018) *AI now report 2018,* pp. 1-62. New York: AI Now Institute at New York University.
36. Zheng, Z., Xie, S., Dai, H.N., Chen, X. and Wang, H. (2018) 'Blockchain challenges and opportunities: A survey', *International journal of web and grid services*, *14*(4), pp. 352-375.
37. Moore, S. (2021) 'Towards a functioning legal framework for emerging DAO technologies in Australia', *ANU Journal of Law and Technology*, *2*(2), pp.109-119.

38. Hao, F., Anderson, R. and Daugman, J. (2006) 'Combining crypto with biometrics effectively', *IEEE transactions on computers*, *55*(9), pp. 1081-1088.
39. Alzakholi, O., Shukur, H., Zebari, R., Abas, S. and Sadeeq, M. (2020) 'Comparison among cloud technologies and cloud performance', *Journal of Applied Science and Technology Trends*, *1*(2), pp. 40-47.
40. Chapman, J. (2015) *Emotionally Durable Design: Objects, experiences and empathy*, 2nd ed. London: Routledge.
41. Ali, S. H., Ayad, H. and Al Rubaie, M. T. (2022) 'Fifth Industrial Revolution (new perspectives)', *International Journal of Business, Management and Economics,* 3(3), pp. 196-212.
42. Kotter, J. P. (1996) *Leading Change.* Boston, MA: Harvard Business School Press.
43. Todnem, R. (2005) 'Organisational Change Management: A critical review', *Journal of Change Management*, 5(4), pp. 369-380.
44. Dai. Y., Li. H., Xie. W. and Deng. T. (2022) 'Power distance belief and workplace communication: The mediating role of fear of authority', *International Journal of Environmental Research and Public Health,* 19(5), pp. 2932.
45. Henry, L. (2008) 'Disengagement and demoralisation: the roots of Ghannian nurses' responses to discrimination in the (UK) NHS', in Tschudin, V. and Davis A. (eds) *The globalisation of nursing,* Oxon, UK: Radcliffe Publishing. (pp.116-127).
46. Hiddlestone-Mumford, J. (2021) 'The Impact of Covid-19 on the use of Strategy and Business Planning to Improve the Viability of a Business', *British Academy of Management Conference, Lancaster University Management School, UK.*

47. Miller, K. (2020) 'The triple bottom line: What it is & why it's important', Harvard Business *School Online,* available at: https://online.hbs.edu/blog/post/what-is-the-triple-bottom-line
48. Weziak-Bialowolska, D., Bialowolski, P., Lee, M. T., Chen, Y., VanderWeele, T. J. and McNeely, E. (2022) 'Prospective associations between social connectedness and mental health: Evidence from a longitudinal survey and health insurance claims data', *International Journal of Public Health,* 67, p. 1604710.
49. Frei, F. X. and Morriss, A. (2020) 'Begin with Trust', *Harvard Business Review,* June 2020, available at: https://hbr.org/2020/05/begin-with-trust.
50. Lehmann-Willenbrock, N. and Allen, J.A. (2014) 'How fun are your meetings? Investigating the relationship between humour patterns in team interactions and team performance', *Journal of Applied Psychology, 99*(6), p.1278.
51. Koshmann, M. A. and Kopczynski, J. (2017) 'Stakeholder Communication', in Scott, C. R. and Lewis. L. (eds) *The International Encyclopedia of Organizational Communication,* John Wiley and Sons.
52. White, S. H. (2000) 'Conceptual foundations of IQ testing', *Psychology, Public Policy, and Law,* 6(1), pp. 33–43.
53. Goleman, D. and Griese, F. (1996) *Emotionale intelligenz.* München: Hanser.
54. Earley, P.C., Ang, S. and Tan, J.S. (2006) *CQ: Developing cultural intelligence at work*. Stanford University Press.
55. Rogers, C. R. (1995) *A way of being.* Houghton Mifflin Harcourt.
56. Bellamy, L., Amoo, N., Mervyn, K. and Hiddlestone-Mumford, J. (2019) 'The Use of Strategy *Tools and Frameworks by SMEs in*

the Strategy Formation Process', International Journal of Organizational Analysis, 27(2), pp. 337-367.

57. Frankl, V. E. (1946). *Ein psycholog erlebt das konzentrationslager.* München, Germany: Verlag für Jugend und Volk. (German).
58. Wallace, J., Hunt, J. and Richards, C. (1999) 'The relationship between organisational culture, organisational climate and managerial values', *International Journal of Public Sector Management*, 12(7), pp. 548-564.
59. Chinongwa, E., Manuere, F., Marima, N. and Mthombeni, A. (2022) 'Psychological factors affecting strategy implementation in organisations. A review of related literature', I*nternational Journal of Research in Commerce and Management Studies* (IJRCMS), (4 6), pp. 92-106.
60. Leyshon, C. (2021) 'How does an individual's culture trigger barriers of communication in a diverse environment? The case of the European Enforcement network an action research inquiry' *Academy of Strategic Management Journal,* 20(2S).

PART SIX

A FINAL WORD

ACKNOWLEDGEMENTS

It really does take a global village to collectively co-create ....

We have so many to people thank for sharing their time, expertise, and support with this book.

A special thanks to:

Zia Brooks for her significant support and contribution on the psychological principles behind mindfulness. Most importantly just being an amazing and insightful person who cares deeply about improving the lives of others.

Maalia Coleman-Leyshon for her significant insights, support and contribution throughout the development of this book. You are so talented, funny, creative and insightful. It would not have been the same without you sharing this journey with us.

Dr. Dermot Kennedy for the forward and provide his case study and glocalisation research findings. We thank him for his great sense of humour, insights and supporting us in this journey.

Damian Grady and Alison Grady for their talent, creativity and passion for creating our incredible balloon head and corporate videos. You are both fantastic people who not only met some intense deadlines but also kept it fun.

Sapna Pierouz our very talented designer, who designed our front cover and created the CQify Branding. She is an awesome person that has supported our project beyond our expectations and always made it fun.

Paul Chappell for the creativity in the illustrations you have enjoyed throughout the book and balloon head animation. He is a pleasure to work with and we had a lot of fun brainstorming the ideas together.

Amy McRae-Johnson our CQify super star who always relentlessly contributes to the project with her expertise in marketing and website design. She is always smiling and we are so thankful for your support, fun factor, and passion.

Kieran Roper for our corporate photography as we immersed ourselves in London's summery locations from across the globe.

Martin Leyshon for taking time off the golf course to provide us with ongoing support, proofreading, and everything else that needed to be done. Dr. Cari Loves you very much :)

Frank Nelissen for your vision, trust, and belief in CQify. It has been an incredible journey so far, with your sense of humor and commitment to this project. We are so privileged to have you on the team.

Travis Cody who has been instrumental in getting this book published with his expertise, vision and enthusiasm. It has been so fun working with you.....now for book number 2!

Connexx European Enforcement Network - a special thank you to everyone who participated in Dr. Cari's initial research and for your ongoing support with CQify.

Our core community of CQify supporters who kindly took time out to provide us with feedback/support at various stages of the development and research for the book (in alphabetical order): Martin Allen, Prof. Naqi Azam, Julie Bagley, Janine LeaBarrett, Fiona Clinton, Mason Coleman-Leyshon, Naz Denning, Karolien Dockers, Geoffrey Galle, Sonia Grant, Gian Lucca Hammerli, Christoph Heller, Samuel Michaelson, Olivia Miklaszewicz, Lawrence Mitchell, Carrie Mosley, Malcolm Mumford, Dr. Kathleen Ngassam, Amanda O-Shea, Andrea Pacini, Prof. Juanita Illingworth, Dr. Yogesh Raut, Dr. Julian Rowa, Michael Watson, Chris Wood, and Bernice van Zutphen.

...and of course, our respective families in keeping us fed and watered, and with loads of cuddles as we wrote.

ABOUT THE AUTHORS

CQify integration strategists and co-creators.

Dr. Cari Leyshon

Dr. Cari is an author, speaker, and founder of CQify.

Cari has over 25 years of entrepreneurial consultancy experience in the UK, Canada, USA, and Europe; with culture change and marketing management using Cultural inQuiry.

linkedin.com/in/dr-cari-leyshon-6212823b

www.cqify.com

Dr. Jacqueline Hiddlestone-Mumford

Dr. Jacqui is a professor, author, and co-founder of CQify.

Over 25 years of senior executive, CEO and Board experience in the public and private sectors complements Jacqui's global academic career.

linkedin.com/in/dr-jacqueline-hiddlestone-34287369

www.cqify.com

Printed by Amazon Italia Logistica S.r.l.
Torrazza Piemonte (TO), Italy

51975415R00179